PASSIVE INCOME RESOLUTION

How an Ordinary Person Built Twelve Passive Income Streams
in One Year (So You Can Too!)

Frankie Calkins

Copyright © 2025 Frankie Calkins

This book was written and created by a human with no assistance from A.I. technologies. Therefore, it likely contains typos, small errors, and imperfections. If you find any issues, please email them to frankie@themoneyresolution.com to help me correct them. On that note, thank you **Justin Doering** for lending your editing skills!

Disclaimer: This book is intended for entertainment purposes only. Always do your research before making any investment or financial decisions. All rights reserved. No part of this publication may be reproduced or utilized in any form or by any means, electronic or mechanical, including photocopying, recording, or by an information storage and retrieval system, without permission in writing from the author.

https://www.TheMoneyResolution.com

Follow "The Money Resolution" and "Passive Income Resolution" on YouTube for inspirational and educational finance videos!

#PIRbook

Dedication

For the dreamers
For the action takers

"Nothing worth having comes easy."
-Theodore Roosevelt

A SPECIAL GIFT FOR YOU

SAVE MONEY RESOLUTION COURSE
Updated and expanded for 2025!

Enjoy huge savings on my course to help you save your first (or next) $10,000 faster than you thought was possible from mindset to action.

You get 2.5 hours of video lessons, a 15 page workbook, a personalized one-sheet planner, slides, and lifetime access.

Get it 75% (!) off with code PIRBOOK
as a thank you for your purchase and support!

Automatically claim your offer at:
https://bit.ly/PIRcourse

TABLE OF CONTENTS

Introduction: Ringtones - *9*

Part I: First Quarter
1. JANUARY: YouTube - 17
2. FEBRUARY: Alternative Investing - 33
3. MARCH: Online Courses - 43

Part II: Second Quarter
4. APRIL: Stock Photography - 61
5. MAY: Voice - 79
6. JUNE: Low-Content Books - 89

Part III: Third Quarter
7. JULY: Affiliate Marketing - 107
8. AUGUST: Credit Cards - 121
9. SEPTEMBER: Self-Publishing - 133

Part IV: Fourth Quarter
10. OCTOBER: Organic Marketing - 151
11. NOVEMBER: Paid Marketing - 165
12. DECEMBER: TikTok - 181

Part V: Recap and Results
13. ONE YEAR LATER - 195

Conclusion: Learn to Earn - 221
Resources: Companion YouTube Videos - 229
Appendix: 101 Best Passive Income Opportunities - 231
A Special Gift For You - 235

Introduction

Ringtones

A USA soccer game was on TV so the bar was more crowded than usual. I found myself in a line of about four or five people waiting to order when the woman in front of me struck up a conversation. She was likely in her mid to late 40s and unusually kind and outgoing (especially for a Seattleite). Eventually, she asked me what I did for a living. I muttered something about being a low-level marketing specialist who recently switched careers from teaching because the pay was so awful. I asked her what she did. What she said blew my mind.

"I'm retired. I do whatever I want!"

"Retired?! How? You look so young!" I said in shock.

"Ringtones. *Look.*"

She pulled out her phone and showed me a chart I couldn't comprehend. It said she made over $500... that day. It was barely 1 pm. I saw the numbers tick up a few dollars in real-time.

"I just made enough looking at that to buy you a beer."

"I don't understand..."

"Years ago I made a bunch of ringtones and chimes and they still sell like hot cakes today. I've been retired for five years living off of passive income." She could tell I was still confused so she clarified, "I make money while I sleep. So, what are you having to drink?"

You know the sound the light bulb above a cartoon character makes on TV when an ah-hah moment hits them? That sound went off in my head. Only for me, it sounded more like the ding a phone makes when you receive a text message. *She probably monetized a similar chime* I thought to myself.

She was still trying to get my order, but I had more questions than answers swirling around my head. How did she make these? Was she a musician? A saleswoman? A ringtone savant?

Nope! She simply paid someone else to do it and sold them on iTunes. She wasn't some top-selling artist, she wasn't a gifted sound engineer, and she definitely wasn't attending the latest ringtone convention to peddle her tunes.

She simply learned how the *"game"* is played.

Stunned I went back to my table of friends, free beer in hand, wishing *I* had enough money to buy all of my friends a round of drinks on me as I briefly fantasized about having my own ringtone business...

More than a decade later I still often think about that woman. How is her ringtone business doing? Is she still retired? My guess is that the ringtone business dried up eventually. I'm not sure if you can still buy ringtones or if iTunes still exists. But I have to assume she figured out a different, better way to earn passive income—I could tell she was savvy. That's just the kind of person she was. She figured out her next ringtones I'm sure.

For years I've been reminded of the retired woman and the day I met her every time I heard another person's phone ring or ding. That day was the first time I learned about passive income and the power it has to change lives—a seemingly random sunny Sunday afternoon in 2012 in the Queen Anne neighborhood of Seattle, Washington after a co-ed softball game. Over the years friends brought up the concept of passive income in conversation and I'd share her story. They'd laugh at how silly the idea sounded.

"There's no way she retired off of ringtones! Real estate is where it's at! THAT'S the only true passive income you can count on!"

I heard enough about real estate for passive income that I looked into it. Sure enough, it sounded phenomenal. There was just one problem: I had no money. In fact I had negative money. I was still a low-level email marketer—a 26-year-old bachelor renting a room in my friend's house that *he* owned. I had a college degree and a master's degree but I had nothing to show for it but a mounting pile of student loan debt. Rest assured, real estate was not in my future plans.

If you picked up this book, I suspect it's not in yours either.

I didn't know how to make a ringtone and I didn't have the money to pay somebody else to do it. Plus, it was probably too late. It was probably too late for *anything*. People like her probably figured out all the easy opportunities by now...

So I went about my daily life, focused on my new career in marketing instead. Eventually, I moved out of my friend's house and got my own apartment. Then I upgraded to a townhouse I couldn't afford. I met a girl and fell in love. We moved into our own one-bedroom apartment. Then a two-bedroom apartment. Slowly, but surely, my life was on an upwards trajectory. But something was always weighing on me. I absolutely saw a future together (marriage, a house, and kids) but I couldn't see it happening anytime soon because of my very negative net worth which now included a mounting pile of credit card debt.

In 2018 I decided enough was enough. I set a one-word New Year's resolution: "Money". I set out to learn all things personal finance from scratch so I could turn my financial life around for good. I admitted to myself that I knew nothing. That had to change, immediately.

I've told the story of what happens next in my previous books so I won't retell it here but, needless to say, things worked out. I *made* it all work out. I forced and willed it to. Failure was not an option. I became financially fit enough to buy an engagement ring, propose, get married, have the wedding of our dreams, go on an exotic honeymoon, and buy a 4-bedroom house near my family where I grew up. All of that happened within a year!

Things were going so well that I set an ambitious goal to retire early. I could retire in my mid-40s like the Ringtone Queen if I set my mind to it. The problem was, all of those life events I just described put a big dent in all of my savings and investing accounts. We also wanted kids (plural), which I knew were expensive, making my dream of early retirement quickly feel like a fantasy.

That's when the light bulb "ding" went off in my head. *Ringtones, Frankie. Ringtones.*

By now you know I don't mean that literally. I mean passive

income.

You don't need to own real estate. You just need your own version of ringtones.

I knew from my year of obsessing over personal finance in 2018 that a person is financially independent when their annual passive income surpasses their annual expenses. Perhaps financial independence wasn't an elusive dream after all. Perhaps I could find my own *ringtones*.

Five years after my first money resolution I set a *new* New Year's money resolution. This time it was two words instead of one: **passive income**. The book you hold in your hands or are listening to is the result of that year. It's my fifth book but I like to think of it as a direct sequel to my first book.

In an effort to uncover my version of ringtones, I created and committed to an ambitious plan for 2023. I was going to become a passive income madman, the way I was a personal finance madman in 2018. Back then I needed to get my financial life in order, get out of debt, save, and invest. This time I was going to make money from nothing. It would require becoming a scientist and anthropologist in the world of passive income. I needed to stop everything else I was doing (outside of my day job) and go all in. Finding my version of ringtones became my mission in 2023. I already had a 9 to 5. I added a 5 to 9—sometimes AM, sometimes PM.

THE PLAN

I committed to creating twelve passive income streams in one year during twelve 30-day passive income challenges. Plus, I committed to documenting everything as I went so I could share my big wins and inevitable losses with people like you—it might make for a good book after all one day! That book might even become a new passive income stream… (There's a lot of meta-commentary ahead so I'm warming you up to that.)

I had some experience with passive income after all. I previously self-published 3 books, recorded my own audiobooks, monetized a YouTube channel, earned a little from affiliate marketing, had a few sponsored videos, and I once made an online course. There are SO many ways to earn passive income and I'd been interested in many of them but never had the time. What would happen if I *made* the time? What was I *really* capable of? This book is the outcome of that curiosity and commitment.

What if you believed in yourself to the point where you knew failure was not an option? What if you believed in yourself relentlessly? What if you let go of fear and negative thoughts? How different could your future look? That was the mentality I had going into it.

My goal for you as you read is to have at least six "ah-hah" light bulb moments—six realizations that will leave you seeing potential every time you hear a phone ring. In the end, I'll share 101 passive income ideas for you to consider pursuing. And remember, even if a chapter is about a passive income stream you have no interest in, the strategies and lessons within each chapter are more important than the income stream itself or results.

I want to emphasize that note about results again: **Do not focus on my income results.** I will share how much I earned by the end of each 30-day challenge at the end of each chapter (if any), and in Chapter 13 I will share my full results, but that's not the important reason for reading this book. Passive income is a long play. And this book is about *you*. Focus on the process and the results will come for you in your own way, in your own time. Do not compare yourself to somebody else that's ahead of you. Compare yourself to where you were yesterday, last month, and last year.

Enjoy the wins, learn from the misses, and embrace the ah-hah light bulb *ding* moments ahead. I'm going to experiment. I'm going to succeed. I'm going to fail. But through it all, we're going to learn a lot together. I hope I find my *ringtones*. I sincerely hope you find yours.

This book is presented with full transparency and in "real-time". I wrote each chapter immediately after each month so I could provide the most accurate version of the details. Buckle up, we're both in for a crazy ride! Thank you for joining me on this journey.

An Important Note Before We Begin

This book is NOT intended to be a sales pitch trying to sell or promote each and every passive income endeavor I pursued. Naturally, I will mention where to find my products or projects but I do so as proof of what I did and for your further learning. If you decide to follow, like, subscribe, invest, take a course, buy another book, or support me financially in any kind of way otherwise, do so at your own discretion. I'm just an ordinary guy obsessed with personal finance, committed to helping you learn how to earn passive income as my number one priority. If you purchased a copy of this book, you have already thanked me for the effort put into this book and my projects. *And for that I thank you.*

With that out of the way, I'll see you in 30 days and a page. Deep breath. I'm jumping right into the deep end...

PART I

First Quarter

CHAPTER ONE

January: YouTube

Can you earn passive income on YouTube in 30 days?
I made 125 videos to find out...

On New Year's Day 2023, I was beyond excited. I was blind with optimism. Yet, 30 days later I felt full of dejection. I was not defeated, but I certainly wanted my new project to start better than it did—especially with all of the hard work I put into it.

I wanted to inspire hope and optimism for the everyday person. What if I end up doing the opposite?

Let me back up to the beginning of the January roller coaster that was YouTube.

For those too excited to read the Introduction, my 2023 New Year's resolution was a big one: Create twelve passive income streams from scratch via twelve 30-day challenges. I'd previously monetized a YouTube channel but the "from scratch" part meant starting over. I had to walk the walk if I was going to provide an honest look at how easy or (more likely) how difficult earning passive income was.

On New Year's Eve, 2022 I posted a farewell video saying goodbye to my 13,000 subscriber YouTube channel. I worked for four years to build that channel into what it was, which included 1.2 million views and $16,000 in income. It may not have been obvious to the viewers but I was fighting back tears when I said:

The title isn't clickbait. This might be the end of The

Money Resolution. I'm taking an extended break and, honesty, there's a chance this is the last video ever. The Money Resolution will not get my attention in 2023. My new channel will. And I'm calling it: Passive Income Resolution.

Here I was the next day, genuinely full of optimism about my new channel and passive income project ahead. I was a man on a mission. I was *going* to monetize a second channel from scratch in 30 days or less. Failure was not an option.

Me and my blind optimism, smugly smiling into the unknown obstacles that lie ahead.

You can see the joy on my face as I posted my first video on my new channel! What a blissful afternoon. It was even a rare sunny day in the thick of winter in the Pacific Northwest. Unfortunately, that's the face of a man who had no idea how daunting the journey ahead was going to be. I sit here in early February wanting to yell some sense into that version of me a month ago.

A challenge to get monetized in 30 days on YouTube and your plan is to make nothing but Shorts? Seriously, Frankie?! Those are brand-new and unproven videos. On a brand new channel? Why not post on your old channel? Why not start with an easier challenge?! Remember when you told your wife this project would take up less of your time than before? Were you lying to her... or yourself?

Okay, enough of the negative inner-monologue guy. The truth is, it wasn't ALL bad. In fact, there was a lot of good about my new channel I'm excited to share!

A POSITIVE START OR FAILURE TO LAUNCH?

As you know by now, my 30-day challenge to monetize a brand-new YouTube channel didn't *exactly* go as planned. I failed to reach my goal of monetizing the channel in 30 days but I did earn passive income! That's a goal I set for myself: earn at least $1 from each challenge before each challenge month ends. A dollar isn't a lot, but it's enough to prove the concept could work passively over time. (I'll share the 30 day income results by the end of each challenge and I will reveal all income results in Chapter 13)

But I don't want you to focus on the money. Not yet at least. This book is about the process. It's about committing and doing the work in a smarter, not harder way. That's the whole idea with passive income. That's what makes it so attractive but there's nothing truly "passive" about it. However, if you do the work right up front, the money will come and continue to come without you needing to do more work. **My definition of passive income** *is earning a disproportionate amount of money for the time and effort put in.* It's the opposite of trading your time for money. That is called a job or a side hustle.

Things were off to a great start. By January 10th, I had already gained 500 subscribers by committing to making 4 Shorts a day, a strategy I'll explain in a moment. 1,000 subscribers is one of the requirements to apply for monetization so I was well on my way to checking the first of two monetization boxes.

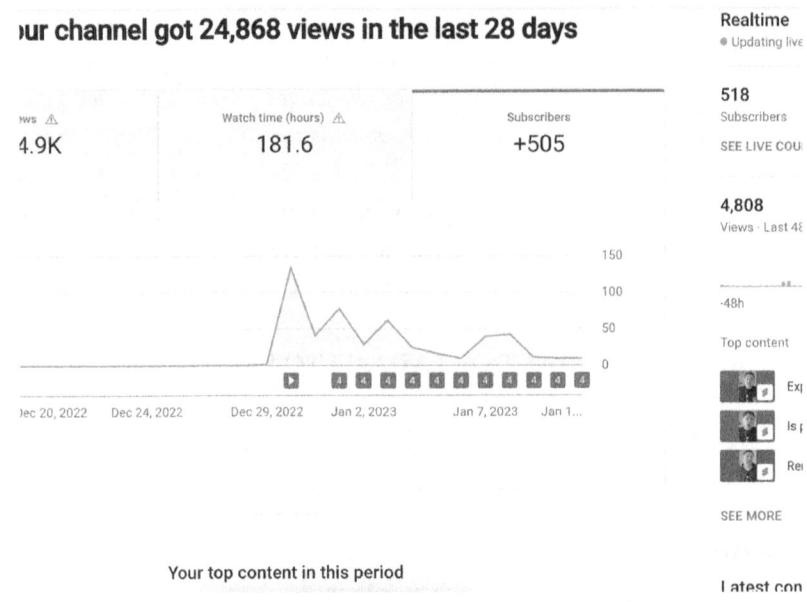

I earned 500 subscribers in less than two weeks!

In fact, if I'm being honest, I was starting to feel overconfident. It took me more than a year to gain 1,000 subscribers on my first channel. I was well on my way to doing it in a month!

Speaking of my first go-round, here's an honest look at what getting monetized on YouTube from scratch looked like for me the first time:

HOW LONG TO PASSIVE INCOME ON YOUTUBE?

With my first channel, I had no idea what I was doing when I started. I didn't even mean to get started. I just finished my first book and I was brainstorming ways to promote it. I decided to post a video on social media announcing I was writing a book. I wasn't sure how to do it but I eventually landed on sharing a YouTube link. One night I said *screw it* and hit record. When the book was available for preorder I did it again. Then again. Then I made a personal finance video that wasn't about my book and I became addicted to hitting the "publish" button.

When I started, I didn't know you could earn money from advertisements. But earning views, then likes, then comments, then subscribers gave me daily tiny hits of dopamine. I was hooked. When I learned you needed 1,000 subscribers and 4,000 watch hours in a 365 day period to get paid passively by turning on ads, I suddenly had a goal. My book was my first passive income stream. YouTube became my second.

It took me 20 months, 10 days, and 74 long-form videos (of poor then average quality) to meet the YouTube monetization requirements. On September 20th, 2020 I was accepted into the YouTube Partner Program. I earned $6.86 from YouTube on September 21st, 2020. The next day I earned $10.77. The next day I earned a whopping $17.23. I was on Cloud 9!

The most exciting $6.86 I've ever earned!

From my research, 20 months is actually fast to get monetized compared to the average YouTube newbie. You should expect monetization to take up to two years and 100 long-form videos. And I do mean longer videos, not Shorts, as I learned the hard way.

I hadn't touched my first YouTube channel *The Money Resolution* for weeks since I posted my dramatic farewell video. I thought YouTube would punish me for a lack of content in January. To my surprise, that didn't happened. As of January 21st, I had 22,000 views, 185 new subscribers, and almost $310 in revenue—metrics that are all on par or above my daily averages, without a single post. YouTube is certainly not passive because it takes a lot of hard work but, in theory, it can be when you take breaks or even step away.

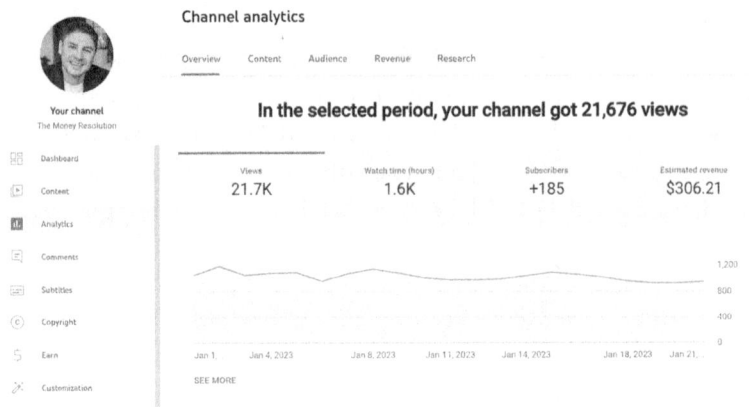

I was thrilled to see I was still earning views and income without posting new videos.

THE SHORTS VS. LONG-FORM CONUNDRUM

YouTube Shorts are vertical videos under 1 minute. They were relatively new in January 2023 and I wanted to experiment by building my new channel in a new way. I wanted to jump on this trend early as I hoped YouTube would bless me with early adopter rewards. After all, I knew it had the potential to grow as big as TikTok.

Shorts was my plan so I stuck with it. But I didn't get lucky or rewarded...

I achieved my goal of making over 120 videos in January—that's over 4 a day. In the end, I published 118 YouTube Shorts. When I realized I was going to need to pivot I also created 7 long-form videos. My YouTube Shorts were a mixed bag of content. Roughly half of them were new content, a quarter of them were content I edited from my first YouTube channel, and a quarter were "Remix" videos, a new feature that allowed you to quickly create Shorts directly from long-form videos.

Why did I start making long-form videos in addition to Shorts? That's because I learned a tough lesson the hard way. I didn't know the monetization rules for Shorts are different than long-form videos (videos over one minute). You need 10,000,000 Shorts views in a 365 day period to apply for monetization. Yes, you read that right. Ten. Million. Views.

If I had taken a moment to seek out updated monetization rules I would have learned Shorts watch hours *don't* count towards the 4,000 watch hour requirement option. So again, you need 1,000 subscribers *AND* 10,000,000 Shorts views *OR* 4,000 long-form video watch hours.

I was devastated when I read this a week into January. How did I miss this? How could I overlook something so simple at the starting line?

Nonetheless, the pivot to long-form mixed in with Shorts got me back on a positive trajectory. By the end of January, I had gained 736 subscribers, 63,000 Shorts views, and 2,000 long-form views. My Shorts gained 336 watch hours. My long-form videos reached 93 watch hours.

I did not reach 1,000 subscribers. I did not reach 10,000,000 Shorts views. I did not reach 4,000 watch hours. In case it isn't obvious, let me be clear: monetizing a YouTube channel to earn passive income in 30 days isn't realistic. In fact, my experiment proves it's nearly impossible. I had experience, I had a plan, I posted daily, and I wasn't even within shouting distance.

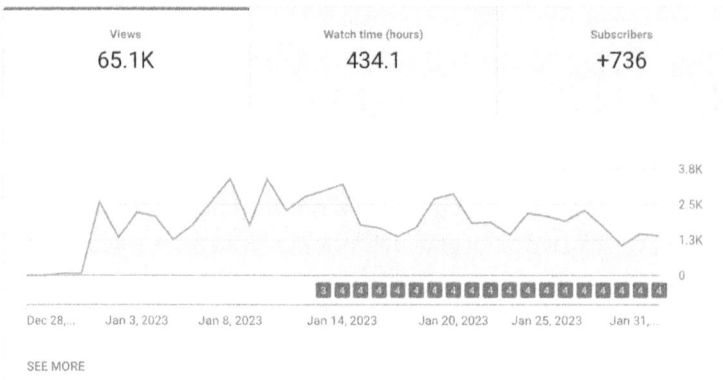

Author's YouTube Studio

My most viewed video was a Shorts titled *Pro Tip for Medium Writers*, which gained nearly 3,000 views. My Shorts video that drove the most subscribers was *2023 Mission: Passive Income*, which earned me 33 subscribers from 1,300 views.

I would estimate that a third of my subscribers were due to the fact that I shared my new channel and project in my final *The Money Resolution* video of 2022 to my 13,000 subscribers. Is that cheating? Maybe. Did it make a difference? Not really. I also emailed my 1,700-person email list about my new project and channel. I likely gained around 500 subscribers from those efforts. I had a leg up but it didn't matter. If it was easy, everybody would do it.

One video viewer described YouTube well when he commented: *Getting to 1,000 subscribers on YouTube must be hellish to reach.* I would edit that to say *Getting to 4,000 watch hours is hellish to reach.* To try to do it in 30 days is setting yourself up for major disappointment.

Ultimately, I'm still very proud of my results. I'm very proud that I had at least 1,000 views every day. I'm very proud that I didn't quit the entire project. In fact, the thought never entered my mind. This YouTube channel could still pay off in a literal sense and become a success story. I know my hard work won't be wasted. But I also know this means posting more videos throughout the year breaking another rule I set for myself: *don't go back to any previous 30-day challenges when the month ends.*

My channel will likely still get monetized. *When* is a big unknown (again, you'll find out in Chapter 13). Would it eventually get monetizing if I never post again? Not at this rate because the two requirements must be met in a 365 day period. However, if I continue making videos about my 30-day passive income challenges, my hope is I'll get there by the end of the year. Deep down I knew this could happen. Eat the frog. Do the hard thing first. Every future challenge should *knocks on wood* be easier from here...

IS YOUTUBE WORTH IT?

Nothing good comes easy on YouTube. You won't get lucky. You have to create your own luck and go all in by showing up consistently. I had an original channel concept by focusing on passive income leveraging Shorts and I went all in. I didn't worry about what my old subscribers, friends, family, or strangers on the internet thought. Apparently, I didn't even worry about reading the new monetization rules!

If you're going to try YouTube for passive income, have an all-in mindset for at least a year. Do I ultimately recommend YouTube to someone brand new to it? Hell yes. But *only* if you set realistic expectations for yourself, have the right intention of helping (or entertaining) others, and have a personal growth mindset. Be open to growth the entire journey because you will learn a *lot* if you are.

WHAT I USE TO MAKE YOUTUBE VIDEOS

If you're considering starting a YouTube channel it might be useful to know what equipment and resources I use to help you get started:

- **Canon M50 camera ($550)**: I upgraded to a DSLR camera after two years, using my first few monetization paychecks to do so. *Cheaper Alternative:* Use your phone! I used my iPhone when I started in 2019. You can and should start there.

- **Rode on-camera microphone ($250)**: I learned that audio is arguably more important than video so I found this microphone and some quick research. *Chapter Alternative:* I reverted back to a basic $80 Audio Technica microphone in late 2022. It's solid, does the job, and even sounds better in some situations. You could also use a lav mic for around $50.

- **Final Cut Pro ($299):** This is a premium video editing software program only available for Apple computers. I found it challenging to learn and managing my storage became a problem. *Cheaper Alternative:* Instead, I reverted back to editing all of my videos using iMovie on my used 2020 MacBook Pro (another cost I shouldn't ignore). Final Cut Pro but it slowed me down. It also costs hundreds of dollars whereas iMovie is free. You can definitely succeed with any program. For example, Davinci Resolve is great and also free.

- **A soft light box ($50):** I was surprised by how much this improved my video quality when I started using one. *Cheater Alternative: Get creative with lamps and leverage natural light from a nearby window.*

- **Epidemic Sound ($120):** This is an annual subscription service for music and sound effects. You cannot use licensed music without permission or your video will get taken down or demonetized. Epidemic Sound provides licensed music you can use with a subscription. *Chapter Alternative: YouTube provides a free audio library for content creators.*

- **Canva ($0):** I have a free account for this online design tool for making video thumbnails.

- **TubeBuddy ($50):** I used this took in the beginning but cancelled it after a year. It's a nice resource to help you create titles and tags but it's not necessary.

- **Pexels and Unsplash ($0):** I get my stock photos for free from these websites. Pexels even has a free stock video library for b-roll!

- **CoSchedule's Headline Analyzer Tool ($0):** It helps me improve titles by giving title ideas a score and tips for improvement. I use a free version but there is a paid version available with more features.

- **Teleprompter and phone app ($30):** I script my videos and recommend doing so. It'll help you speed up your video editing 10-fold and provide better value to viewers with easier-to-follow videos. Get a teleprompter and teleprompter app and practice getting comfortable with the setup. I thought everyone would know I use a teleprompter. They don't. *Spoiler: Most YouTubers do the same!*

I've spent around $1,300 over four years of creating videos, but I regret spending at least a third of that. You really can start with just your phone and a $50 microphone. Prioritize audio over video in the beginning. People will watch a low-quality video with great audio. They won't watch a 4K video with bad audio.

All this is to say: don't overthink equipment or use that as an excuse to not start. You don't need paid subscription services or fancy equipment. Do some personal research, start before you're ready, niche down into one topic to find your audience, and learn as you go!

WHAT DID I LEARN?

YouTube will teach you a *lot* if you're committed to the process and show up consistently. Here's some of what I learned about YouTube and about myself during my first passive income challenge 125 videos later.

In terms of YouTube, I learned the YouTube monetization rules inside and out (eventually), including new changes related to Shorts videos. I also learned YouTube is *not* oversaturated and it's *not* too late—my friends often ask me about this. I learned the YouTube algorithm is predictably unpredictable. Don't let that discourage you. Finally, I learned how to analyze available YouTube data constantly and from different angles to uncover different stories and opportunities.

Personally, I learned how to prioritize creating content daily, how to be more confident on camera, and how to stop trying to be perfect. I learned to stop trying to be other YouTubers. There's only one of me. *Why be anyone else?* I learned how to tell stories in my videos by establishing the stakes, building up a conflict, and paying it off in the end.

I learned I enjoyed documenting my daily progress in a journal because it held me accountable. I also found out my creative super weapon is running. I ran over 50 miles in January outside during the winter in Washington State (rain or clouds) because I realized it was helping me unlock creative ideas and push through.

I already knew this but I was reminded that my wife is the most supportive person in the world—if you're in a relationship, YouTube requires a supportive partner! I learned to appreciate every small win because the highs are high but the many lows are very low (*Hooray! I worked hard for hours and hit publish on a great video! But nobody watched it…*). Finally, I found out how much I can learn and how much fun I can have when I push myself to do something extremely difficult. *That was the best part.*

What could you learn? What skills could you gain? And what might you learn about yourself? Imagine your growth if you went all in on YouTube for a year. Will you get monetized and earn passive income in 30 days? Most certainly not. But it's a fantastic place to start your passive income journey. You can find your voice, document your journey, hone your skills, and find your audience. You'll also hear feedback in the comments that can shape future passive income projects. Plus, you'll experience and understand the power of those daily dopamine hits!

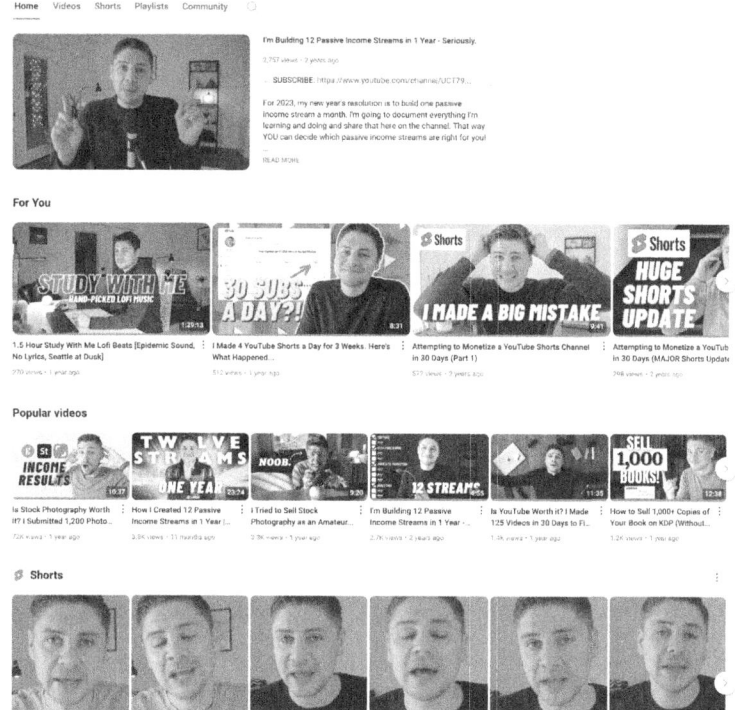

A look at my channel homepage two years later (with hints at what's to come in the chapters ahead!)

JANUARY PASSIVE INCOME RESULTS

This YouTube challenge was my first of twelve attempts to build passive income streams. It may take me a year or more to earn passive income from YouTube but January wasn't a total failure from a passive income perspective. As a backup, I also started a new Patreon which I mentioned in several videos throughout the month. I earned 4 subscribers in January that paid me $17 in passive income.

Earn at least $1 in January: mission accomplished.

My Patron URL is patreon.com/resolution if you're interested in subscribing or observing how I set it up. If you subscribe for as little as $1 you'll see exactly what my subscribers saw throughout the year. The big sell was my in-progress Google Sheet with tabs documenting all of my notes for each challenge and an income chart for each month.

My new Patron page!

If you're starting a YouTube channel my advice is to have fun. Make mistakes. Laugh at yourself. Celebrate successes. Have a long-term growth mindset. Smile and be confident—even when you're faking it at first. Don't think about the money—that will come and be a bonus, a literal passive income bonus each month for years to come.

But also, *don't wait*. The best time to start YouTube was yesterday. The second best time is today.

Just.

Press.

Record.

Questions for Reflection: If you said screw it and hit record right now as I did in 2019, what would you talk about to share on YouTube? What topic do you know well enough to teach? What hobby are you passionate about enough to talk about for hours? Ideally, who would you be speaking to? What lessons can you learn from my mistakes and successes? As a reminder, you can get my full passive income planning Google Sheet for additional resources and a template to use for your journey at https://bit.ly/passiveincomesheet

CHAPTER TWO
February: Alternative Investing

The case for alternatives is very intriguing, especially with the always looming potential recession ahead...

Alternative music.
Alternative fashion.
Alternative investing?!

That was my February passive income challenge. As it turned out, after some initial research and set-up it was hands-off and fun! What more can you ask for?

What are alternative investments? They are financial assets that are not considered to be traditional investments such as stocks, bonds, or cash. They range from art to real estate to cryptocurrency.

The goal: Double my money by the end of the year. My hypothesis: The right alternative investment found via intensive research could lead to a disproportionate amount of income compared to standard stock investing. The mission: Dive deep into the world of alternative investing to decide how to invest $500 into alternatives to set myself up to earn passive income.

COLOR ME SKEPTICAL

I had always been pretty skeptical about alternative investing—or as those in the know call them: "alts". Perhaps that's because some of the biggest investment crazes turned mostly into flops in recent years (case in point, NFTs). However, after researching alts for weeks, I have to admit I quickly found legitimate reasons to pursue alternative investing.

First, the big appeal for alts is that they are a hedge against a down market. That's because they work independently from traditional markets like stocks and bonds (for the most part). Alts can zig while the stock market zags. And in early 2023, the stock market had been zagging. That made alts especially attractive because the word "recession" had been floated around a lot. Then again, when hasn't it? Having alternative investments in addition to traditional assets in your portfolio could protect you from market volatility.

Further, most will find alts far more interesting than the dusty ol' stock market, especially if they align with their personal interests. Alts aren't new but their rise in popularity and ease of access is. According to the market research firm Preqin, the total dollar value in these classes has more than doubled between 2015 and 2021 and is forecasted to reach $23 trillion by 2026. That's *trillion*, with a *T*!

It does seem logical that alts will continue to rise because again, technology is making it easier than ever to invest in them. Fortunately, alternatives are no longer reserved for the top 1% of the wealthy. Thanks to technology and advancements in the finance industry, you now have access to highly sought-after non-traditional investments.

But even after a few weeks of researching, I still wasn't a full believer in alternative investments. After all, this was my hard-earned money I was about to part with and I'm always very careful before investing. I had a great deal of skepticism throughout my research and you should too! **Always do your own research** before blindly following the advice of anyone, including me.

Are alts a wise investment? Is now the right time to get in? Or are they going to become the latest investment craze that slowly fizzles out in a few years? I can't answer these questions yet, and that'll ultimately be up to you to research and decide, but let me tell you more about what I do know about investing and why I ultimately did part with $500 in the pursuit of passive income the alternative way.

BREAKING MY INVESTING PHILOSOPHY

I'm a self-proclaimed self-taught money nerd. I prefer 'nerd' over 'guru'—it's way less pressure, and I can still geek out over dollar signs without pretending I have all the answers! Think of me as that friend who's spent way too much time reading about compound interest and gets a little too excited about budgeting spreadsheets.

As a part of that mission to learn all things money from scratch, I studied everything I could about investing. I learned what to do and, more importantly, what NOT to do.

My investing philosophy is simple:

1. Invest in everything.
2. Do it consistently.
3. Do it automatically.
4. Do it as much as possible.

Everything means the total stock market (or S&P 500 if I'm feeling frisky).

Consistently means dollar-cost averaging.

Automatically means automated each paycheck so I don't have to think about it.

As much as possible means max out all of my tax-advantaged retirement accounts—for me, that's a 401K, Roth IRA, and HSA. I invest even when it feels painful in the moment to!

I make those decisions ahead of time so emotions get in my way. I don't hand-pick individual stocks. I don't invest in the hot new thing. NFT's? In my book, it stands for **Not F-ing Touching**! My investment strategy to date is boring. But boring works! Every good book about money agrees—including all of mine!

The only time I strayed from my trusty investing plan was during those, well, let's call them 'moments of curiosity.' Fine, you got me—it wasn't just once but twice that I took a plunge into the wild world of cryptocurrency. Yes, I'm talking about Bitcoin. Okay, you caught me again—it was Dogecoin too. What can I say? Even the best-laid plans sometimes get sidetracked by the lure of digital gold and meme coins.

Long story short, it didn't go well. I lost *half* of my investment in less than a month... twice! The first time was after trying to invest in Bitcoin right after the first massive value spike. I showed up first in line for the fall! The second time was via Dogecoin on the day Elon Musk hosted SNL. What a fun night that was. If you know what it's like to desperately catch a train or bus that has already left the station, you know this feeling!

This all explains why I've stayed away from alts until now. If I was set in my investing approach and I learned the alternative investing lesson the hard way twice, why did I pursue alternative investments as part of my passive income strategy?

I'll tell you why.

It won't make sense.

The logical money nerd in me won't enjoy admitting it out loud.

But, if you want to know the truth...

It's because it's the opposite of boring.

It's kind of exciting! And it's super interesting when you dig into it!

I found out you can combine your investing with hobbies and interests and make money doing so?! Was this some kind of financial magic trick? Was this money wizardry? Had I died and gone to compound interest heaven?!

I might be exaggerating but that's the honest truth.

I dipped my toes into the alternative investing pool because it got me excited. It was fun. At the very least, I knew it would make for good YouTube content and a chapter in a book—*I hoped*. Plus, based on what I learned a week into my February challenge, alts might be a good idea after all.

If creative investing meant investing in cars, wine, hotel skyscrapers, gold, whisky, baseball cards, insanely beautiful art, and even the sport of pickleball... take my money! Take it, then double it and send it all back! Please and thank you.

Fool me once, shame on Bitcoin. Fool me twice, shame on Dogecoin. Fool me thrice, maybe alternative investing just isn't for me. I guess we'll find out! So, alternative investing—is it legit or is it a scam?

Color me skeptical. Color me excited!

MY ALTERNATIVE INVESTING PLAN

In February I took $500 that I saved up and I invested $100 into five alternative investments via five alternative investment platforms that I hand-picked. I was able to do all of this online fairly easily. I decided to stick with $500 to limit my exposure and to see if I could double a relatively small amount of money. Here's what I ultimately invested in by the end of February, 2022:

1. Real Estate Crowdfunding

This is one of the most popular alternative investments. Real estate crowdfunding connects investors with real estate builders or buyers looking to loan your money. With real estate crowdfunding you're essentially the "bank". You loan money in exchange for interest payments, plus a return on your original investment.

The barrier to entry can be low. $10 might get you in the door so you can claim ownership to a small sliver of a property (that single square inch belongs to me!). While some real estate investment platforms are only open to accredited investors, many are available to the masses. The best platforms vet the rental properties, vet the renters, do home maintenance as needed, and collect rent when it's due (or handle a flip).

All you do is select which rental property you want to invest in, buy shares in the property, and earn passive income. Platforms to consider are Arrived, Fundrise, Crowd Street, and Groundfloor.

An alternative (yet a more traditional investing approach), would be to invest in a REIT—real estate investment trust. You can typically invest in REIT within your main investing platform. A REIT likely offers lower risks and lower rewards.

Investment #1: I started with what is popular and felt relatively safe. That led me to real estate and crowdfunding. I used Fundrise to invest $100 into a standard fund they offer.

2. Peer-to-Peer Lending (personal loans)

Peer-to-peer lending is an alternative investing strategy where P2P platforms connect borrowers directly with lenders and cut out the middleman. The P2P platforms set the terms, and individuals looking to borrow are pre-qualified. Some sites focus on bigger, riskier returns, while others focus on consistent, minimal returns.

You need to know your appetite for risk, and research the recipe from there. As with most alternative investments, there is the risk of losing everything with peer-to-peer lending. The people who are borrowing your money may not have the best credit, so you run the risk of never having your money repaid.

There are many peer-to-peer platforms but start by looking into Lending Club, PeerStreet, and Prosper.

Investment #2: I dove into peer-to-peer lending, once again because of its popularity. I landed on Prosper as my platform of choice because it's one of the oldest and most trusted P2P sites. I invested $100 total into two, low-risk loans.

3. Collectibles

Collectibles aren't just dusty trinkets on a shelf—they can accumulate some serious value over time. Why? Scarcity and special interests.

But this value depends on the rarity and, especially, the condition, and this is harder to find than you might think. For example, a friend of mine grew up playing Pokemon and had a Base Set 'Shadowless' Charizard literally worth around $5,000 when it's in 'mint' condition. Unfortunately, it was shiny enough to enjoy playing with, so the card was basically destroyed, and (besides the nostalgic value) worthless.

Regardless, for me, collectibles are where passion meets profit, assuming I'm old enough to avoid playing with the expensive collectibles. That said, passion does make it hard to take emotions out of decision-making. Once again, I recommend you only invest money into collectibles that you are willing to lose. You could make a lot, or you can lose it all so start small and tread cautiously.

There aren't many easy ways to invest in collectibles online but I recommend the platforms Collectable and Rally.

Investment #3: *I went with Rally and I ended up loving the platform. It's easy to use and addictive to browse your favorite categories. I was most drawn to nostalgic products, art, sports cards, and random historical artifacts so that's what I invested my $100 in.*

#87ZELDA - '87 NES LEGEND OF ZELDA
Cost Basis: $7.50 (1 Share)
Avg Cost: $7.50 per share
Value: $9.00 ($9.00 per share)
Your Gain/Loss: +20.00%

#WARHOL1 - '67 ANDY WARHOL MARILYN MONROE PRINT (SIGNED)
Cost Basis: $9.00 (1 Share)
Avg Cost: $9.00 per share
Value: $8.25 ($8.25 per share)
Your Gain/Loss: **-8.33%**

#DEATON - TRICERATOPS SKULL "DEATON"
Cost Basis: $16.00 (1 Share)
Avg Cost: $16.00 per share
Value: $15.55 ($15.55 per share)
Your Gain/Loss: **-2.81%**

#1776 - DECLARATION OF INDEPENDENCE
Cost Basis: $36.85 (1 Share)
Avg Cost: $36.85 per share
Value: $41.15 ($41.15 per share)
Your Gain/Loss: +11.67%

A handful of my investments. I also invested in a mint condition Ken Griffey Jr. rookie card.

4. Wine & Spirits

Like most alternatives, the value of wine is independent of the economy and consumer trends. Plus, the performance looks solid. According to Entrepreneur, this non-traditional investment has yielded a 13.6% annualized return over the last 15 years.

Just like my friend's forgotten Charizard, certain bottles gets better with age—both in taste and value. Having an understanding of different wines and which years were good vintages is important. Proper storage is also very important so the wine doesn't turn to vinegar.

Luckily, you don't have to be a sommelier to get in on the action. There are wine and spirit investing platforms that do the legwork for you. They identify good wine, help educate you, store the wine, and insure the wine. Plus, with some platforms, you can choose to simply drink your investment if you'd rather! But if you do, it won't taste like profit I promise.

The platforms I recommend are VinoVest and Vint.

Investment #4: My wife has a sommelier certificate so it was a no-brainer to invest in wine. I wanted to use VinoVest but the minimum was out of budget. Research led me to Vint. I invested $100 into a rare burgundy bundle.

5. Small Business Debt

This alternative caught my eye for similar reasons as collectibles—I find it interesting! As an entrepreneur myself (and someone who appreciates platforms like Kickstarter), I love the idea of investing in new small businesses, especially if you can find them locally.

By investing in small business debt, you can invest in your community and help business start-ups succeed. Brick-and-mortar business examples include breweries, restaurants, coffee shops, dispensaries, and more.

Mainvest is a platform I recommend and enjoyed browsing. I found dozens of stores on the platform across the US, and even some in my backyard. Alternatively, you can invest in venture capital via platforms like Sweater.

Investment #5: I loved the idea of investing in a small business. I found a taproom an hour and a half away from my home on the platform Mainvest. I invested $100 into the business and plan to attend their grand opening in a *couple of months. Fingers crossed for a free drink for a VIP investor!*

FINAL THOUGHTS

Other alts I researched and considered were art, farmland, and commodities (such as gold). For more, you can watch deep-dive videos into my collectible investment using Ralley as well as my wine investment on my new *Passive Income Resolution* YouTube channel. My Vint wine investing review video was also my first sponsored video on my new YouTube channel! The videos are titled: How to Earn Passive Income from Rare Collectibles and Fine Wine Investing for the Everyday Person.

Alternatives are unique and fun, they're more accessible than ever, they're a hedge against a down market via diversification, and they can work as a hedge against inflation. On the flip side, liquidity can be low and they are risky—there is no guarantee you'll earn money. In fact, you could lose money. Only invest with money you're willing to lose and do not invest in alts as any kind of retirement plan or even short-term passive income plan. I view alts as a fun way to earn a little passive income while supporting hobbies, businesses, and individuals trying to improve their own lives. Invest cautiously, stick with what you enjoy and understand, and again for the fourth time say it with me: *only invest money you are willing to lose.*

> ***Questions for Reflection:*** *As you learned about passive income from alternatives and explored my choices, did you find yourself excited about unique investments or are you more risk-averse? Have you ever lost money from a unique investment? Do you have money you're willing to lose? Do you already have a solid traditional investing plan for retirement? If you answered no to either of the last two questions, alternative investing may not be a good fit for you!*

CHAPTER THREE
March: Online Courses

Your mini-course blueprint to course launch success

In late 2020 I made and published my first online course with little effort, no money, and no idea what I was doing. To my shock and surprise, it launched to commercial and critical success!
Did that really happen?
Nope!
Creating my first video course *Save Money Resolution* was months of hard work—a true labor of love. It launched to crickets. I remember announcing it on my first YouTube channel with a short video trailer promising viewers that I knew the secret to saving $10,000 *fast*. One of the first commenters said *"A course? Already?"*

Point taken. Who the heck was I? Little ol' me. A nobody at the time to be sure. Yes, I was close to my first 1,000 subscribers on YouTube but looking back, it seems I got a little carried away. I got swept up in the passive income hype I had been devouring from books, YouTube videos, and podcast episodes for months on end.

Nevertheless, I did launch a course in 2020 alongside my shiny new website. It was an intense three months of hard work. I spent around $2,000 to make it, mostly on website and video hosting fees. I rarely missed a day working on it.

On launch day I excitedly shouted to my then-girlfriend now wife, "If just one person buys my course today we're going out to dinner on me!" I might have even said, *"**When** the first person..."* I saw her eyes light up. In that moment I realized how brutal it would feel to let her down, let alone myself.

Luckily, I made a sale an hour later!

I quickly ran to my computer to confirm it was real. It *WAS* real. I clicked the email alert to find the name of the person who bought it. The email address looked familiar... it was my mom. That counts for *something*. Was it worth a dinner celebration? Probably not, but a promise is a promise.

I spent the dinner desperately checking my email alerts. *Surely someone else must have ordered something? Aunts? Uncles? A high school teacher?*

More crickets.

Everybody on YouTube and podcasts said this would happen but I didn't believe them. Now I was living it. Blind optimism morphed into denial as the first of five stages of grief set in.

One more person bought my course in the first 30 days. It was indeed a total stranger but I had already accepted my course was a failure. A second dinner celebration didn't exactly seem appropriate. It was months of wasted effort and lost time.

Flash forward two and a half years. I've made $460 from my first course. Again, that's *something*! That's enough to cover four dinner date nights out. (I still play this internal game when it comes to passive income. I figure out what expenses my passive income is able to cover each month. It started as covering a $10 streaming service subscription in the beginning. Most months it now covers my utilities. My dream is to earn enough to cover my mortgage! The dream of financial independence is always with me.)

Alas, it's a new year. It's a new month. It's a new opportunity. I learned a lot from my mistakes, which is why I still don't regret making my course before I was ready. To this day, I'm proud of my website and overall course content. I still think the content holds up very well but there's a lot I would improve if I could do it all over again (*foreshadowing*). I've learned enough about creating and promoting online courses to create something worth watching.

Before I cover my March challenge process and results, here are the top lessons I learned from creating *Save Money Resolution* two years ago.

COURSE LAUNCH TIPS FOR SUCCESS

When I reflected back on my first course, I still stand by the creation process, the content, and my course platform of choice. There's a lot I would do differently if I could do it all over again *(foreshadowing)*. I simply didn't have a clue how to sell the damn thing. I didn't have a big enough audience or even small group of superfans. Here's what I did right and wrong to help you avoid crickets at launch:

Nail your topic

Your topic of choice is critical for success. That probably goes without saying but honing in on the perfect topic is easier said than done. What topic do you know well enough to simplify and teach? Reflect on what friends and family come to you for help with and why. What questions do they ask? *Those are major clues.* It doesn't matter how big or small the question or issue is. If you help a specific group of people overcome a problem and find a solution, that's a sign that you have a desirable skill or knowledge in demand. Your knowledge might be desirable enough that people are willing to pay you to teach them, no matter how big or extra specific.

Teach one-on-one

Teach your skills or knowledge to real people. **Do it for free.** They say if you're good at something, never do it for free. But sometimes you have to! That way you can make sure it works! It also helps you identify your method, determine what to avoid, and find your overall voice (without the pressure of making it worth someone's money). This was invaluable to me. I offered finance coaching for free. I did this and it helped me understand what people needed help with the most. I learned most people wanted help tackling credit card debt or finding a way to get out of the paycheck-to-paycheck cycle and actually save money.

Survey the people

You *must* validate your ideas. The best way to do so is to ask! Before I made my course I made a four-question Google Form survey. I asked about financial topics that interested people (saving money was #1). I also asked what they'd be willing to pay, how long the course should be, and about the number one financial problem they wish they could solve. Keep it brief—five questions or less. Aim for 50 or more responses. Include an open-ended question where people can share more thoughts. Then take the results to heart! Put your biases aside and listen *carefully* to the data. My issue in 2020 was not trying hard enough to get more responses. I ended up with 27 survey responses. That's a good start, but too small of a sample size for tangible results.

3. How much would you personally be willing to pay for each outcome? *	<$50	$50 - $100	$100 - $200	$200 - $500	$500+	N/A (no inte...
Save Your Fi...	☐	☐	☐	☐	☐	☐
Get Out of C...	☐	☐	☐	☐	☐	☐
Invest Twice...	☐	☐	☐	☐	☐	☐
Build Your Fi...	☐	☐	☐	☐	☐	☐
Increase Yo...	☐	☐	☐	☐	☐	☐
Learn Everyt...	☐	☐	☐	☐	☐	☐
Develop & A...	☐	☐	☐	☐	☐	☐

One of the questions on my survey

Collect email addresses

While my survey was great, I forgot to ask for email addresses at the end of my survey so my warm leads suddenly became ice-cold because I had no way to contact them. Explain why you're collecting their email—it's to let them know when the course is available and to offer a discount. It's also an opportunity to send a personalized thank

Passive Income Resolution

you note, which I recommend. Build goodwill. Use it to sell later.

Tip: Consider offering an incentive such as a $5 gift card to Starbucks for all survey responders or run a raffle. Trust me, this cost will pay off. It's worth it to spend a little bit of money to gather key data points and email addresses!

To create the course content, start with the end in mind

What will the desired transformation and end result be for the course taker? If your course doesn't have a desired transformation or end result, you're not going to deliver value. If it has no value, you'll have a hard time selling it. Back into the steps as modules and lessons from there. To help my students save $10,000 I brainstormed 50 concepts. Then I organized my ideas into seven categories that later became my modules. I decided on four lessons per module which required me to cut nearly half of my ideas and only keep the best. Then I got to work writing my lessons and video scripts.

If you get stuck creating the content, ask yourself: *What would I tell a friend or loved one as advice?* If you know the subject well enough to teach it, the answers should come naturally.

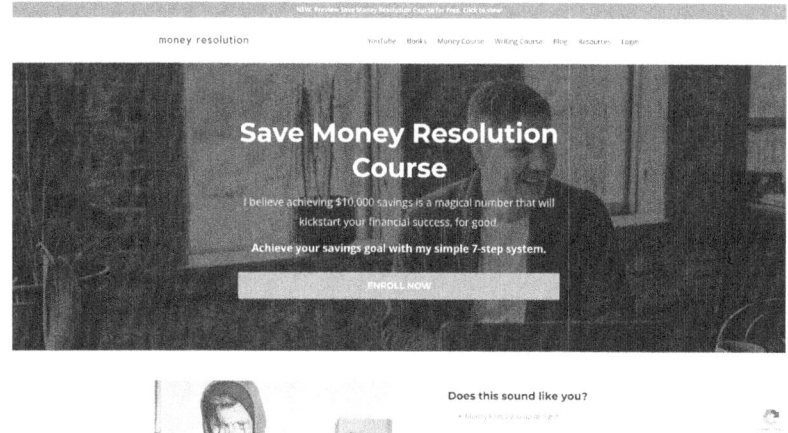

My course website: https://www.themoneyresolution.com

Create a quality landing page

I decided to use Kajabi for my course website because an all-in-one solution that gave me full flexibility. It's not cheap but it included a website, marketing tools like email, site metrics, and more. I scoured the web to find the best course sites as examples. I took screenshots of my favorites. I sketched out a wireframe for what I wanted to build. Then I built it using simple drag-and-drop tools.

I was very happy with how it turned out. On your website, include as much of the following as you can: where your work has been featured, testimonials, the course outline, everything included with the course, an FAQ section, price, and a quick video trailer.

I gave away Module 1 for users that got to the bottom of my sales page and still felt unsure about purchasing

Don't undersell your value

Many course creators suggest you price your course much higher than you think you can sell it for. I'm talking *thousands*! This can give your course more prestige and make it more desirable. However, thousands sounds crazy to me unless your name is Dave Ramsey or Tony Robbins.

Alternatively, if you price your course too low, it won't look valuable and people might be skeptical about the quality. To decide on a price, I referenced my survey data. I landed on $97. I also included a full no-questions-asked money-back guarantee because it's better than a negative review. I suggest you give the beta version of your course away for free in exchange for testimonials. Then launch at half off to get students in the door.

My price page with included materials

Make a mini-course instead of one masterclass

I made the common mistake of trying to do *too* much. I wanted to make a 5-hour masterclass. This is excessive, especially for your first course. Plus, people want results quicker! Eventually, I cut out half of my content but it was still two hours long. I should have made it a one hour or less mini-course and focused on a short-term outcome. For example, save $1,000 in 30 days priced at $29. Another mini-course idea I could teach is: *How to create a debt payoff plan*. That's an achievable outcome within a week. If you're making a course about baseball, you could teach: *How to steal a base*. You shouldn't try to teach *How to win the World Series*. Some course creators even have a dozen mini-courses. A great example is Miss Excel. She offers dozens of mini courses, but she also offers bundles if you want all of the courses for a discount.

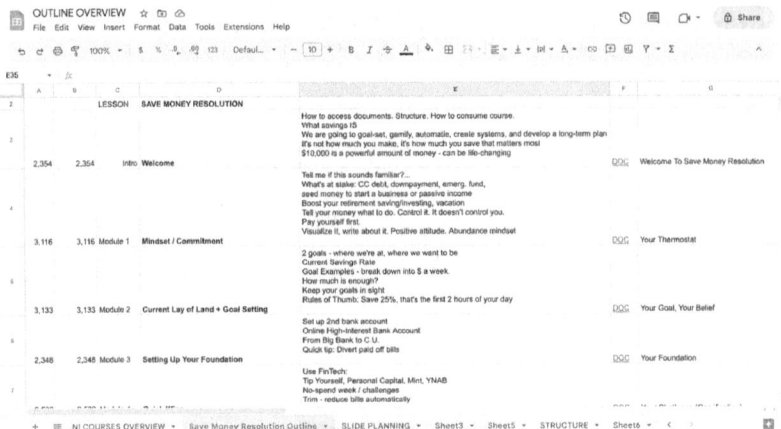

My original planning sheet with far too many ideas.

Create a course marketing plan

If you build it, they don't just come. You have to market yourself and your course. I should have waited until I had 1,000 email subscribers, not 100. I should have launched when I had 10,000 YouTube subscribers, not 1,000. How to market your course could be a whole course itself (ironically many people offer them) but here are some quick ideas:

- Learn to master social media ads or Google ads.
- Answer questions on a related topic on Quora or Reddit and promote your course at the end.
- Write related blog posts on your site or sites like Medium and promote your course within it.
- Write a short ebook and offer a discount on your course at the end.

Either way, don't wait until launch day to figure out a marketing plan and *hope you get to go out to dinner*. Mom might support you, but others likely won't. A marketing plan is critical. This is why I dedicated two future chapters to it. In Chapter 10 you'll learn about free marketing strategies. In Chapter 11 you'll learn about paid strategies.

Refresh and relaunch

This is perhaps my most important point. It's what brought me to try this again after all! Your first course is an experiment. It won't be perfect. You get better with experience. That difference between a mistake and a lesson is perspective, and your perspective here depends on your willingness to change and try, try again. That's what builds experience—not hoping to strike gold by digging in the same hole you started years ago.

Take a step back, observe your environment, try out some new shoveling methods, and find a new place to dig!

Why not take that experience and feedback and make your course even better? A relaunch is one way to revive a dead course. Add content. Add bonuses. Give it a fresh coat of paint. Refilm it when you have more camera confidence. Create slides or worksheets to include if you didn't the first time. You can even relaunch on a new course platform or an additional course platform.

MY COURSE FACELIFT AND RELAUNCH

I didn't intend to relaunch my course in March. This felt like cheating in my challenge because I'm supposed to take on each monthly challenge "from scratch". However, when researching for my new course I started by reflecting on my first course. I dug into my Kajabi course data and watched some of my course videos back, putting myself in the shoes of a student. Frankly, I felt a little embarrassed about what I saw. When I filmed my course, I wasn't confident on camera and it showed. I didn't display any enthusiasm. The video quality and content weren't the issues. *I'm the problem. It's me.*

How can I expect people to pay for a course when the course creator has trouble getting through it?

I took a deep breath. I knew what had to be done before the real challenge began. I needed to refilm and re-edit the entire 2-hour and 20-minute course. I couldn't help myself. I needed the delivery of the lessons to match the quality of the content. Refilming it alone would have been a huge undertaking but I also decided to update the course content itself. I cut the fluff. I added tips. I updated the resources. It needed to be perfect because I'm *definitely not* making this course a third time. After a week of rewrites, the scripts were polished and ready.

During the second week of March, I refilmed *Save Money Resolution* over two days after work. Editing the videos took me another two days. Uploading the new videos to Kajabi and making some edits to the course landing page took another day. But *presto!* My new and improved course was live on my site mid-month and I was very happy with it.

I didn't stop there because I still need to promote and sell it! When I reflected on how hard it was to sell my course the first time I realized it was because I hosted it on my own website where very few people could discover it. Therefore, I decided to put my new and improved *Save Money Resolution* course on a dedicated course platform to see if I could reach and help more people. After all, some of these sites help promote quality courses to their built-in audience of course lovers!

I landed on Udemy over many others like Teachable, Thinkific, and Coursera mainly because it has a massive marketplace dedicated to courses. In fact, Udemy has nearly 50 million users worldwide! Plus, it's the simplest way for anyone—yes, even you—to make and launch a course for sale online. I wanted exposure to that marketplace. By putting my course on Udemy, it was like putting my product on the shelf in the popular course supermarket where the buyers are already shopping.

The pros: Udemy is very easy to use, free to use, and you can set your own course price.

The cons: Udemy takes 63% of all course sales unless sign-ups use your specific referral link. They also put courses on sale quite often. Plus, the Udemy approval process takes several days and there are course rules and restrictions you have to follow. For example, I couldn't reference "money" in my title or description which is pretty hard considering my course is all about saving money.

Needless to say, by mid-March my updated course was now live on my website, and the renamed *Save 10K Fast Masterclass* was also live on Udemy. I even made a new course trailer to help promote the relaunch. Mission 1: Accomplished.

My New Course Creation and Launch

Now the hard part: it was finally time to **create and launch a brand new course**, ideally on my site and Udemy as well. Here is my step-by-step process from brainstorming to publishing:

Step 1: Brainstorm

Right away I thought of a dozen or so course topics. The ideas ranged from paying down debt, self-publishing a book on Amazon, starting a YouTube channel, writing on Medium, building a Kajabi website, how to use iMovie, email marketing, and even fantasy football for beginners. I narrowed it down to two topics:

Option 1: Self-publishing on Amazon. I previously self-published 3 books and it's what people ask me for help with the most. Plus, I enjoy teaching the topic and it's where my online content creator career started.

Option 2: Writing on the platform Medium. I've posted close to 200 articles and I'm now earning as much on Medium as I make on YouTube in a year. Plus, it's easy for anyone to use and get started.

I went back and forth a least a dozen times. Ultimately, I landed on a Medium course for two big reasons. First, with Amazon Kindle Direct Publishing there was a *lot* to cover. I only had time to make a mini-course. Further, I already had a Medium audience I could sell a course to! I previously made a few YouTube videos about Medium and one of them recently crossed 85,000 views. Smartly, I promoted a Medium tips PDF guide during that video which is gated by an email sign-up form on my website. I had already gathered over 900 email addresses of people interested in writing on Medium! Plus, I could post about my course in the video description of all my old Medium videos that still get views.

Step 2: Determine the course focus

Following my own advice, I decided to survey my audience. I emailed my list of 900+ Medium email subscribers asking them to take a 5-minute survey. I also posted an article on Medium asking Medium writers to take the survey as well. All told I received 23 survey completions. This wasn't as many as I was hoping for. I should have made the survey and questions shorter. I should have given out those Starbucks gift cards! Regardless, there was value in the data I did have. One theme definitely stood out: *How to make money on Medium*.

Step 3: Create my course outline

I wanted my mini-course to be around 1 hour long. My first course was 7 modules with 4 to 5 lessons within those. I decided to make this course 5 modules with 2 lessons or less in each. My quick math showed that would get me close to one hour.

To create the outline I needed to think about my audience and even the course title. Unfortunately, my survey takers were all over the map. Some were looking to get started while others had been writing on Medium for years. I decided to make my course for every Medium writer. That might have been a mistake but I had to make decisions quickly. The title needed to hint at "making money" without saying "money" (per Udemy's rules). I wanted it to be appealing to beginners and experienced writers struggling to make money. I landed on: *Medium Income Quickstart Masterclass: How to get into the Medium Partner Program and earn $100+ a month consistently*

Earning $100 in a month sounded like a feasible goal. I also didn't want to overpromise and underdeliver. I landed on these five topics for my five modules:

1. Medium editor basics and tricks
2. Writing and editing tips
3. Medium secrets and hacks
4. 20 free writing resources
5. How to make money on Medium

Step 4: Write the course lessons

I figured out the course needed to be around 10,000 words because my 2-hour and 20-minute course was 22,000 words. Since it was 5 modules I needed to write one 2,000-word module a day Monday through Friday. This made it feel a lot more doable. Luckily, I worked way ahead of schedule because I knew the topic so well. Plus, I was working off a great outline I made via Google Sheets I created in the last step.

On Monday I was on fire. I wrote Module 1, 2, and most of 3. On Tuesday I finished Module 3. Then Module 4 and 5 poured out of me immediately after. On Wednesday I wrote the introduction, Conclusion, and course trailer script. I also edited the script. On Thursday I edited the entire course... a second time. Then I decided to go for it and I began filming. I tried to film it all in one sitting but I ran out of steam after a two-hour session. On Friday I finished filming and jumped straight into editing the videos. It was much easier to edit than a standard YouTube video because the videos didn't need bells and whistles such as music, sound effects, stock videos, and the like. On Saturday I wrapped up editing and started uploading to Udemy. On Sunday I finished the Udemy submission process. On Monday of the following week, I uploaded the course to my Kajabi website as well.

I was exhausted. I was *done*.

All told I went from brainstorming to publishing a new mini-course on my website and Udemy within 9 days. But how did I market it and did it sell?

Step 5: Promote and sell the course

I promoted the course to my 900+ Medium person email list. I promoted it to my 23 survey takers via email. I even promoted it to the remaining 1,100 subscribers on my email list who probably didn't even know what Medium was. I posted on social media and wrote an article about the course on Medium. I also made a video trailer and posted it to YouTube.

I launched my Medium course for free to get people to take it. I needed reviews and testimonials before I charged. My plan was to increase the price slowly over the next few weeks and months. 30 people joined the course on my website in the first 48 hours! I upped the price to $5 on day 3 and I made $25 in the first 24 hours at that price point. Not too shabby.

The Udemy course took longer to get approved but 221 people joined the course in the first 24 hours because it was free. This earned it a special badge as it became the #1 course about Medium. Plus, the first review was fantastic!

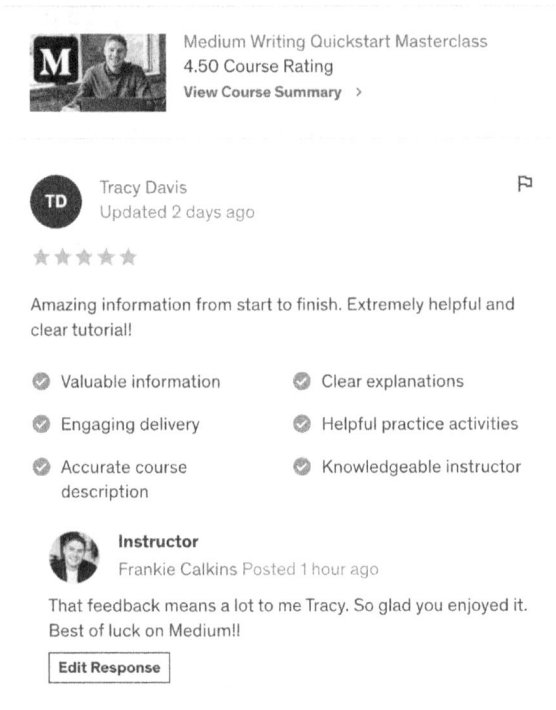

Be sure to reply to your reviewers, especially if they aren't 5-stars. Say 'thank you' or ask for feedback for improvements.

MARCH PASSIVE INCOME RESULTS

Since I already had equipment from my YouTube channel, creating my courses didn't include any expenses. How much did I earn? In the first couple of weeks after relaunch my Save Money Resolution course earned $165.20 from 6 new students. Admittedly, I wasn't able to promote it as much as I normally would have because I moved right onto my new course creation. Speaking of, my Medium course earned $71.03 from 236 new students. Clearly most of those students were able to take advantage of the free launch price. Best of all, I'm proud of both courses and stand behind them. Plus, all but two Udemy reviews have been 5-stars, which means the content is useful and resonating with others.

I hope you feel inspired because there are people who are willing to pay for what you know. Online courses might be the future of education. They're here now. They're here to stay. They're a great way to earn passive income online. And you can make a course better and faster than you probably thought if you're committed and passionate about it! I proved that to myself this month.

Look for my mini-course about mini-course creation soon! I'm only kidding. I'm out of time and energy…

Three challenges were complete. My YouTube channel still wasn't monetized. I wouldn't earn passive income from my alternative investments for some time (those are a long play). But I now had *two* courses I'm proud of on two different sites. Plus, I was up to seven Patreon subscribers. April was the challenge was most looking forward to! I always wanted to try my hand at stock photography! I'll see you in 30 days and a page!

Questions for Reflection: What do your friends and family ask you for help with? What topic do you know well enough to teach? Where do your passions and interests align with knowledge most people don't have? What result have you produced for yourself that others would desire? These questions can help you brainstorm your specific topic and audience for a course if and when you're ready to make one!

PART II

Second Quarter

CHAPTER FOUR
April: Stock Photography

Light bulb, digital camera, take action!

I've always been very interested in trying my hand at photography. Over the years, I've often found myself going on walks with the sole purpose of taking photos. On trips I've always been that person who takes way too many pictures—you know, the must-capture-every-moment type. So naturally, with a family trip to Mexico on the horizon, I figured, why not turn my obsession into something that could actually make me money?

In April, I spent 30 days trying my hand at taking, uploading, and selling stock photography. I wanted to find out if a total amateur with no experience could earn passive income from stock photography because I often see it mentioned as a top passive income opportunity. In fact, I've recommended stock photography a time or two over the years on YouTube.

In this chapter I'll share:

- My photo-taking process, early challenges and photography goal
- The sites I chose to use to list my photos
- What went right and sometimes very wrong
- Top tips and what I wish I would have done differently
- How much passive income I earned by the end of the month

CAPTURING THE BEAUTY OF MEXICO

Armed with my Canon M50 camera, I decided I'd use the beautiful backdrop of Mexico to try my hand at stock photography for real. The trick was balancing it with the whole being on vacation part. I didn't want to be that person ruining family fun by constantly fiddling with my camera.

So I came up with a plan: I'd get up before the sun every morning and head out on one to two-hour photo missions. I wandered the resort, explored the beaches, checked out the golf course, strolled through town—basically, if it looked interesting, I was there snapping away. One morning, I even hiked up a cliff to catch the sunrise, which felt a little like living in a postcard.

Sunrises are difficult to photograph but beautiful to watch!

I looked forward to my morning walks daily. It was in no way a chore since I wake up with or before the sun most days anyway. It was peaceful, I got steps in, and I saw amazing scenery I wouldn't have otherwise. *Zero* complaints. Bringing my camera worked out well for two reasons. First, the resort, nearby golf course, and beach were stunning—the area was extremely photogenic. I got a lot of beautiful shots, especially at "golden hour". Second, I also took close to 100 candid shots of the family that I'm sure we're going to cherish for a long time. I'm not going to post the family shots to stock sites but there's nothing like quality vacation photos from a nice camera. Speaking of…

IS A NICE CAMERA REQUIRED?

When I say "nice camera" I should clarify that mine isn't fancy or expensive. In fact, I was worried my entry-level camera might hold me back. As I mentioned, I've used a Canon M50 camera for the last few years for my YouTube videos. I rarely pull it off the tripod and take it outside but I did exactly that throughout April.

I also spent time trying to learn about taking quality stock photography from YouTube videos and podcasts. Funny enough, some very successful photographers swear by iPhone photos. One person put out a poll of the same photo side by side with a nice camera vs. an iPhone and most people couldn't tell the difference. At one point during the month, I did start taking some iPhone photos and I even submitted some older iPhone photos I already had but I'm getting ahead of myself…

I found a "natural" photo setting on my Cannon M50 and I stuck with it for the most part. It gave the photos a more organic look to them. Plus, I heard you can do a lot more with organic-looking photos in color editing.

My wife being a good sport.

MY STOCK PHOTOGRAPHY PLAN

My original goal was to take 1,000 quality photos throughout April. That's how many photos I planned to edit and submit for approval to stock websites. Ideally, I hoped to get at least half of those photos approved and uploaded to be sold. When you do the math 1,000 is roughly 33 quality photos a day. That's a lot as a goal but I started off strong! 10 days into April I came back from Mexico with 550 photos. Around 400 of them were quality in my humble, untrained opinion.

The bad news was the next 600 were going to be a lot more difficult and take a lot more creativity. Back home, it took me 10 more days to shoot another 100 photos, putting me halfway to my goal with 10 days to go. I needed a plan for the next 500 photos so I made one. I came up with a fairly generic shot list. It was more of a location list but it was massively helpful. A plan always is. Failure to plan is planning to fail.

Shot list
Vespa
Night market
Ruston way - DONE
Chambers bay
Downtown Tacoma
Chihuly bridge
Point Defiance Zoo?
Leo - DONE
Desk set up?
Mall/shopping
Waterfront - DONE
Seattle...
Stadium HS
Food
Vashon Island

Older Camera Photos:
Aruba
Sunriver
Seattle day

Use any older thumbnail shots with M50?

My shot list after returning from Mexico

I didn't have anything specific in mind. I simply wanted to go to interesting places in my hometown Tacoma, Washington, and nearby Seattle. I sought out places I knew I'd enjoy exploring that had potential for interesting shots.

I also dug up photos from our Aruba trip that I took with the same camera on our honeymoon and added a few random photos from my iPhone. *Presto*! A few days later I had another 200 shots. 700 wasn't 1,000 but I was very proud of the effort. Plus, if my original goal was 500, I would likely only have 400 or 500 photos tops! Set your own bar high. You know, shoot for the moon and such...

EARLY CHALLENGES

Editing my Mexico photos was a learning curve. I could level them and crop but I didn't know how to "color edit". I imported the photos into the Photos application on my MacBook Pro and used the auto-enhance feature for most photos. The photos looked great and improved but it was actually compressing the photos. The stock sites I chose to upload photos to required the photos to be 4MP or more and auto-enhance was making them 2MP to 4MP tops. There would be no easy button. *Rats.*

> mall. Images must be at least 4 MP and vector previews at least 15 MP. Lear

My first roadblock. Also, what's a vector preview?!

I had to pivot and hunt for a different photo editing program. I found a dozen or so that were free but I couldn't decide which to try. *Hint: too much research leads to info overload and analysis paralysis.*

Let me explain because I found myself in this familiar route almost every month when doing these challenges. I was in deep—scouring through forums, reading reviews, and comparing features. Before I knew it, I had fifty tabs open, each promising to be the "best free editor." There were too many options, and the more I read, the more confused I became. Should I go with the one that's highly rated for beginners? Or the one pros use but with a steeper learning curve? And then there was one with a sleek interface but half of the features were locked behind a paywall.

It's that classic trap of over-researching: you think you're being productive, but in reality, you're spinning your wheels. You become so bogged down by options and trying to make the "perfect" choice that you end up making no choice at all.

Eventually, I had to step back, close most of those tabs, and just pick something. I finally chose Adobe's Lightroom because I intended to upload to Adobe and it had a nice integration to import from Lightroom directly. I really enjoyed Lightroom. However, it does cost $9.99 a month after a 7-day free trial. Luckily, a free trial was all I needed!

TAG, I'M OUT!

With a week to go, I quickly realized the fun part was over. The real work was ahead of me. I won't cover all the upload process details here but here's the gist: After carefully editing each photo I had to upload the photos to two different sites—I chose Adobe Stock and Shutterstock. Then I had to categorize, title, and tag every photo individually *twice* because I was submitting to two sites.

Tagging was easily the most tedious part. You can add up to 50 tags or keywords to each photo. I figured it was best to add 50 tags to improve searchability. Luckily, you can add and edit tags in bulk, plus there are some AI tools built into the sites to help, but it's still very tedious and time-consuming.

Thank goodness for AI tagging suggestions!

I lost steam and time after days in the upload process and I set a new adjusted goal of uploading 600 of my best photos onto both sites.

As I finished up I realized I had a major blind spot. I ignored stock video. In research I learned video is where the biggest opportunity is to earn passive income. I gave it a shot (pun intended) in Mexico but I wasn't pleased with my early results. None of the videos felt good enough to submit, mostly because they were a little shaky. I meant to pull out my tripod when I got home to try again but I totally forgot. Funny enough, when I compared my Canon M50 stock videos to videos from my phone, I realized the iPhone would have been a better filming option from a quality perspective. Again, food for thought.

ADOBE STOCK SUBMISSION RESULTS

Adobe Stock turned out to be a tough nut to crack. Of the 585 photos, only 32 were accepted by the end of April. *Ouch.* To add salt to the wound, Adobe took its sweet time reviewing my photos—it was much slower than platforms like Shutterstock. In fact, two weeks after upload there were still 185 photos in review.

One of the most frustrating parts? Adobe offered zero feedback when they reject your photos. I had no idea what I was doing wrong or why my photos weren't making the cut. Based on some quick math, I predicted I would end up with around 50 photos accepted and listed when my final batch is reviewed. (*Several entire batches of 50+ photos were fully rejected early on. It was extremely demoralizing and it's one of the big reasons why I decided to stop at 600 submission.*)

My Adobe Stock portfolio

ADOBE STOCK INCOME RESULTS

Did I make money with my 32 photos within a month of uploading my photos on Adobe? *Nope. Zero. Zip. Zilch.* I imagine it'll be hard to earn more than a few dollars a year from Adobe. Based on my experience so far, I cannot recommend uploading stock photos to Adobe Stock for income if you're an amateur like me. Of course, you may have better luck, and I may have more luck with these photos in the future (Spoiler: I do! As a reminder, the full results will be revealed in Chapter 13), but you can see I clearly didn't have success in April.

My sad, empty Adobe Stock dashboard

SHUTTERSTOCK UPLOAD RESULTS

Shutterstock was a whole different ball game compared to Adobe Stock—I finally saw some real progress! Out of the 576 photos I uploaded (a few ran into technical issues, so I had to leave out 25), a solid 260 were accepted. That's *five times* more than Adobe's approval rate, which was a huge confidence boost after my earlier struggles.

With a 45% acceptance rate, I was pleasantly surprised, and I'll admit it felt like validation after all the setbacks with the other platform.

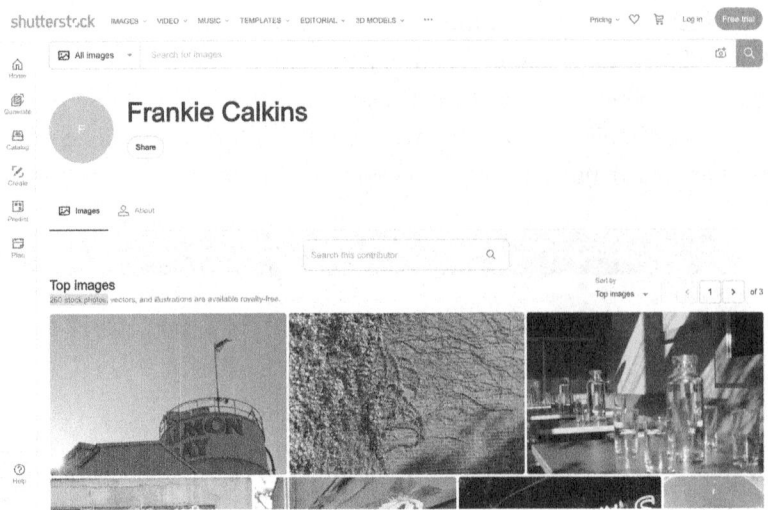

My Shutterstock portfolio

The only downside to uploading to Shutterstock was I did frequently hit an upload cap but I simply needed to wait 24 hours to submit more photos. Shutterstock also seemed to have a more streamlined and faster review process. Unlike Adobe, I wasn't left hanging with submissions in limbo for weeks. Best of all, Shutterstock actually provided feedback for each rejected photo. Here is some of that feedback so you can try to avoid making the same photography mistakes.

FINDING EVERY WAY TO GET REJECTED!

First of all, you can't have any kind of trademark or intellectual property shown in your photo. This photo got rejected for a visible brand name or logo (I still haven't found a logo—though I'm sure they're right):

Rejection reasons (1)
Visible Trademark: Content contains visible brand names or logos.

I learned graffiti is considered intellectual property. Makes sense!

IMG_0050.JPG

Rejection reasons (1)

Intellectual Property: Content contains subject matter that potentially infringes on intellectual property rights (e.g. artwork, writing, sheet music, isolated modern architecture, or other objects protected by copyright).

Some photos were rejected for missing model releases from people and landmarks.

Rejection reasons (1)

Missing Model Release: A model release is required for this submission but was not provided.

Some photos were rejected for the main subject being out of focus.

IMG_1279.jpg

Rejection reasons (1)

Focus: The main subject is out of focus or is not in focus due to camera shake, motion blur, overuse of noise reduction, or technical limitations of the equipment used (e.g. autofocus searching, camera sensor quality, etc).

Some photos were rejected for needing an English translation.

IMG_1324.jpg

Rejection reasons (1)

Translation Required: An English translation is required for non-English text that appears in content. For small amounts of text, please provide translations in the title field. Large amounts of text are not allowed in content.

Some photos were rejected because they were under, over, or inconsistently exposed.

Rejection reasons (1)

Exposure: Content is underexposed, overexposed, or is inconsistently exposed.

Some photos were rejected for noise and artifacts.

Rejection reasons (1)

Noise / Artifacts: Content contains noise, film grain, compression artifacts, pixelation, and/or posterization that detracts from the main subject.

This is one of my favorite photos I took in April but it was rejected because I gave it a bad title. Apparently "Vacation travel in Loreto, Mexico" wasn't descriptive enough. That's fair.

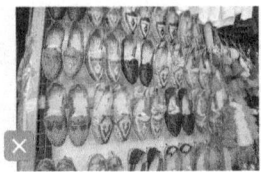

Rejection reasons (1)

Title: Title must be descriptive and relevant to the subject matter and must be in English. Titles cannot contain special characters, spelling/grammar errors, or repeat words/phrases in excess.

Most photos were only rejected for one reason but a few bad apples reminded me how amateur I really am with three or more rejection reasons.

IMG_1990.jpg
2294182857

Rejection reasons (3)

Missing Model Release: A model release is required for this submission but was not provided.

Intellectual Property: Content contains subject matter that potentially infringes on intellectual property rights (e.g. artwork, writing, sheet music, isolated modern architecture, or other objects protected by copyright).

Visible Trademark: Content contains visible brand names or logos.

SHUTTERSTOCK INCOME RESULTS

Did I make money on Shutterstock during my 30-day project? *I actually did!* I was very excited when I logged in on April 26th and saw I had one download that was going to pay out $0.30. I had one additional download the same day for $0.10. I earned a whopping $0.40 in April. My goal was to make at least $1 but I still call the challenge a success because I did reach $1 earned a week later. My stock photography project wasn't a rousing success but it also wasn't a total disaster! Here are the two photos that were downloaded, both were shot in Mexico.

Asset ID	Lifetime download count	Lifetime earnings	Upload date
2293681931 Image	1	$0.30	04/25/2023
2293665721 Image	1	$0.10	04/25/2023

MY TOP 7 STOCK PHOTOGRAPHY LESSONS

Here are the key lessons I want to ensure you take away from my project, especially if you are considering diving into the world of stock photography for passive income:

1. There are lots of site options to choose from to upload your photos for sale. Choose wisely!

There are micro and macro stock sites. Macro sites are much tougher to get selected into. Some examples are Offset and Getty Images. I decided to upload to microsites which are easier to get selected into but there's more competition and the pay is going to be less (unless you take phenomenal photos that break through the noise).

2. When it comes to video and income, the 80/20 rule applies.

The 80/20 rule, also known as the Pareto Principle, is the idea that 80% of results come from 20% of the effort. It's a pattern you see in many areas, and stock photography is no exception. For example, if you upload half photos and half videos, 80% of your revenue (or more) will likely come from stock videos. Further, 20% of your stock videos will make up 80% of your total video income. Since I use my camera to shoot my YouTube videos, I thought I could use my camera to shoot quality videos but I was lacking an auto stabilizer feature.

3. Lighting is critical.

The sun can be your best friend (natural light) or enemy (shadows or oversaturation). Unfortunately, we had the wettest, coldest April in history in the Seattle area so that didn't bode well for getting outside and getting great shots. People need gloomy shots too, right?!

4. Color editing is hard.

I wasted a lot of time going down the filter preset rabbit hole in Lightroom. Generally speaking, that led to a lot of analysis paralysis and overthinking, slowing me down. A part of me wondered if I should have uploaded without editing so users could manipulate the raw photos how they wanted. Needless to say, I haven't figured out how to approach editing without spending an unscalable amount of time on it. It might be worth looking into AI tools that could help you.

5. Speaking of hard, the upload process is extremely tedious.

Once you take a good photo, edit it, and upload it, you still have a lot of work to do. You need to categorize each photo. You need to name each photo. Most importantly, you need to tag each photo with up to 50 tags. Tags are how people find your hard work. Think of them as keywords that make your photos searchable; without them, your images might get lost in the sea of stock photos. Skipping this step isn't an option, but tagging can be incredibly time-consuming. Luckily, many sites have AI tools that help you add tags easily—though they can be hit or miss. You can also select multiple images and add tags at once. Lean on any and all shortcuts during this step of the process.

6. Release forms are a big deal.

If you have any recognizable people or landmarks in your photo, you must have a release form and you must upload that with your image. Otherwise, you'll see a red notice because the sites definitely require it. I didn't want to deal with release forms so I focused on nature and inanimate objects. One day I expanded to pets, and by pets I mean my dog. Every day is an opportunity for a great shot! I took this photo at a nearby park and it sold!

Photo taken by author of his dog Leo who was also a good sport

7. Most of all, this project has taught me to be intentional with my photos.

I didn't want to spend days upon days choosing the best photos from a group so, when I took a photo, I only took one. This has spilled over into everyday life when I'm taking photos day to day. I used to take a dozen so I could find the perfect one later but then I'd never go back and find the perfect one. Sound familiar? Being intentional helps you save time. Use that time to live in the moment more!

FINAL THOUGHTS

Even if I didn't make a full dollar, the project wasn't a failure because it was a lot of fun! Personally, I'm thrilled to have hundreds of amazing photos from our trip of family I'll cherish. This challenge also encouraged me to get out of the house when I was back home. I got exercise, I definitely learned a lot and improved skills, and there's a chance I actually earn some money over time! Do I recommend stock photography? Yes, but only if you have realistic expectations.

Try Shutterstock or a few other sites that look promising to you. Have fun with it. Focus on gaining skills, not money. And stick with quality, not quantity. Upload 20 to 50 of your very best photos to 4 or 5 sites, see what you learn, and go from there.

If you do want to earn money, consider avoiding all the hassle I just described and stick with stock video only. Video is where you could really succeed, especially if you have people in them who are willing to sign model release forms. As someone who is always looking for quality stock videos for my YouTube channels, I can tell you there's high demand!

I'll emphasize this point again: have fun! Fun has been a theme so far with all four months of passive income challenges. It's important you have fun and enjoy what you're doing when you're building passive income streams. That's because building passive income streams is very tough to do and having fun helps you forget how much work you're putting in. Fun helps you stay motivated and focus. Fun makes the hard work feel that much more rewarding.

It should be obvious by now that income from stock photography is unlikely in the short term (especially in 30 days). But it's a long play! Don't forget, we're investing our time and efforts now for future payoffs—put int the hard work today and earn with little to no future effort required. Perhaps it should be called *"active, then passive income income"*. Either way, with 4 challenges complete, my momentum entering May was high. The question is, could I keep it going? Here are my questions for you to get you going!

Questions for Reflection: What photos or videos could you take around your house or neighborhood? Are there everyday moments you overlook that might actually make great stock photos or videos? Do you have friends or family that would be willing to "model" for photos and sign release forms? Is there a different hobby other than photography you've always had your eye on that you might be able to monetize?

PS: Life is beautiful. Take more photos of it all.

CHAPTER FIVE
May: Voice

Is this the most underrated passive income stream?

For my May 30-day challenge I took on a passive income project I had been meaning to complete for a year and a half—finally record the audiobook for my third book, *Save Half, Retire Fast.* This book became my best seller after all! (I also wondered if there were other ways of earning passive income from voice gigs I wasn't aware of…)

I previously recorded audiobooks for my first book *The Money Resolution* and my second book *Money, You Can Hack It,* but those books were much shorter: 140 and 190 pages respectively. My third book was nearly 300 pages long! That's roughly 70,000 words, hours upon hours of reading into a microphone, and countless takes to get the phrasing just right. Not to mention, reading my own work aloud feels like reliving every moment of the writing process all over again—for better or worse.

I finally committed to working through the entire process, and I'm excited to share the detailed process. You would think making an audiobook got easier each time. It didn't. I learned many new lessons the hard way you need to know if you're consider trying your hand at income from audio. But I also had fun!

It was a month of hard work, but I was thrilled to submit the audio files and get my audiobook approved by ACX (Audiobook Creation Exchange). The best part is, ACX automatically lists audiobooks on Amazon, Audible, and even iTunes. Those sites are where you can officially find my new audiobook!

In this chapter, you're going to learn:

- How much money you can realistically make from audiobooks
- How to record an audiobook
- My personal top tips and tricks
- How you can be an audiobook narrator and earn passive income (even if you don't have your own book)
- Plus, other ways you can earn passive income from audio!

AUDIOBOOK INCOME POTENTIAL

How much can you expect to make from audiobooks? I can't answer that for everyone but I'll share my numbers as an indie-author. When I created my first audiobook I had no audience and no idea what I was doing. It became available on May 8th, 2019. Roughly five years later, I've sold 180 units and earned 0 bounties, which you earn if people sign up to Audible using your referral link. According to ACX, you can earn up to $75 for each referred member that remains a member for at least 61 days. I've never promoted my link but you definitely should! It was a miss on my part.

My second audiobook was published on April 13, 2021. Roughly three years later, I've sold 81 units. All told, between my 2 audiobooks, I've sold 261 units. That's around 65 units a year or roughly 5.5 a month.

Here's how my 261 sales break down via my full sales dashboard in ACX:

- 162 sales are AL Units which are audiobook units bought by Audible Listener members using their membership credits. I earn 25% for AL Unit sales.
- 60 sales are ALOP Units which means audiobook units bought by Audible Listener members not using their membership credit. I earn 40% of ALOP Unit sales.
- 39 sales are ALC Units which means audiobook units bought by customers that are not Audible Listener members. I earn

- 40% of ALC Unit sales.
- And -1 was a return.

Title ▲	Author Name	On Sale Date	AL Units	ALOP Units	ALC Units	Qualified Return Units[1]	Net Sales Units	Bounties Earned
Money, You Can Hack It: 101 Creative Ways To Increase Your Net Worth, Grow Your Wealth, and Have Fun Along The Way View on Audible | View on ACX	Frankie Calkins	13 Apr 2021 UTC	58	7	16	0	**81**	0
The Money Resolution: 101 Ways To Save Money, Make Money & Get Out Of Debt In One Year View on Audible | View on ACX	Frankie Calkins	24 Apr 2019 UTC	104	53	23	-1	**179**	0

My full sales dashboard via ACX

As an example, if you earn 40% of the revenue on a $20 book you earn $8 a sale. Unfortunately, you can't control your final Audible price. My first audiobook is currently on sale for $5.99 and my second audiobook is listed at $17.35. They are supposedly priced based on length, but it can vary and shift so my hunch is it's also based on sales and popularity.

It took some digging (ACX didn't include a convenient historical sales dashboard) but I downloaded and examined all of my ACX monthly reports to determine my total income from my two audiobooks; I earned a grand total of $1,250 from 261 units sold. That's $4.79 a unit. Let's round up for simplicity and call it $5 a unit.

Anecdotally, I make around $25 a month from my 2 audiobooks. I do nothing to promote these so it's *completely* passive income and a nice surprise when it hits my bank account.

HOW TO RECORD AN AUDIOBOOK

Counting my new audiobook, I have recorded all three of my

audiobooks using GarageBand, a free program for Mac users. Other programs I've seen recommended are Audacity, Adobe Audition, ProTools, Twisted Wave, Studio One, and Reaper.

You don't need an expensive microphone to record an audiobook. I recorded my first two books with an $80 microphone by Audio Technica and a $10 pop filter (these reduce the popping sound "p's" often make when you speak). You do need a quiet room because background noise will cause your files to get rejected by ACX during the upload process. Most people aren't aware of how noisy their house or computer are! Years ago I had to re-record several chapters because outside rain was picked up by my microphone. Also, be aware of room echo. Hang sheets or drapes to deaden the sound. As a hack, consider recording in a closet. The hanging clothes actually help reduce all room echo!

The finished audiobook was 37 chapters and 44 total recordings when you include the Introduction, Conclusion, References, Bonuses and such. Here's a look at what my final Garage Band file looked like:

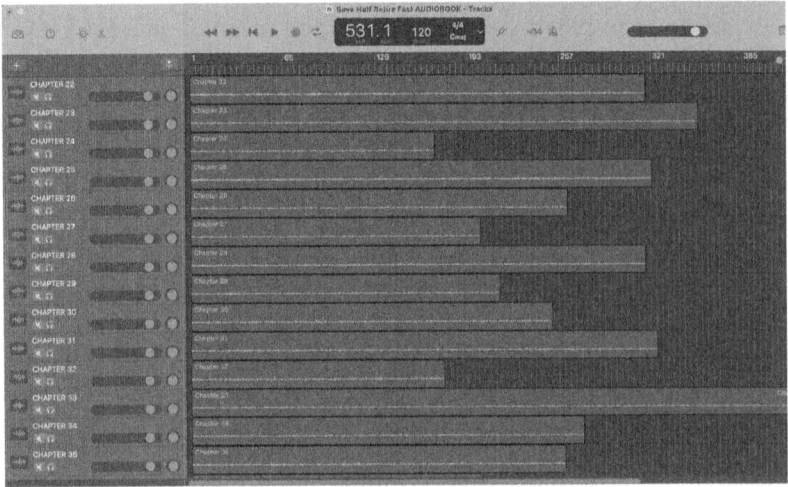

This is only a THIRD of the final file...

THE RECORDING PROCESS

The entire recording process can be tedious and time-consuming.

My new book ended up being close to 7-hours long. By my estimation, it took 14 additional hours to edit, export, upload, and master the tracks to meet Audible requirements (I believe 'master' is a fancy word for 'edit').

How long will it take you? Let's try some math! My book was 72,000 words and 7 hours long. I estimate it took me one hour to record 10,000 words. Next, triple the book page length to determine the total time commitment. For example, a 40,000-word book would be 4 hours long. The total audiobook project time commitment is 12 hours. It could be less if you outsource the edit process. It could be more if you're learning as you go, especially if this is your first audiobook!

About this Title   **Produce Audiobook**   Audiobook Sales

UPLOAD MANAGER   AUDIO ANALYSIS

Full Production - 6 hrs 52 mins 56 sec*
*Current running time, which does not include the retail audio sample

Welcome to the Production Manager! Use this space to upload the audio files fi organize files for delivery.

If you entered chapter names while setting up this project, we've populated them matter ('Table of Contents,' 'Dedication,' etc.) and back matter ('About the Author audiobook. If you don't customize your chapter names here, names will default to

You'll have so much fun listening you'll wish it was 10 hours!

I recorded my first two audiobooks in one *very* dedicated weekend for each book. I recorded the audio for each book first and edited the files immediately after. During the month of May, I tackled three to five chapters at a time in the morning over 3 weeks and I edited most nights in the evening. It was nice to break it up over time but eventually, I wished I had just locked myself in a room for a weekend again because it felt like I was barely making progress during most of the month.

I also ran into several audio issues at the time of upload for the first time. It took me 6 or 7 hours to fix all the tracks, re-export, and re-upload when I thought I was done. But I learned a lot about compressors, limiters and noise gates! The ironic part about my new issues is that I invested in a new Shure MV7 $300 microphone to improve my audio quality. Unfortunately, I didn't have the settings dialed in before I hit record. Again, you might want to outsource the editing process. However, if I kept it simple as before with my simple microphone, I probably could have coasted through the editing stage without the snags. You don't have to be an audio technician, but you have to be the kind of person that likes to problem solve and push through when challenges arise!

IS RECORDING AN AUDIOBOOK FUN?!

I explained the commitment and a few challenges but is it fun at all? It can be! There is an element to reading aloud that lends itself to delivering a performance, which I enjoyed. You should focus on enthusiasm with your voice to keep it interesting for the reader and yourself. Plus, I had fun going back through my book that I hadn't looked through in over a year. I consistently felt proud of the book and its content! I'm sure I'll experience the same when I (eventually) record the audiobook for this book!

As a bonus, recording the audio for my book also helped me find several typos. In fact, I found 40+ small typos. I wrote them down as I recorded. When I finished the audiobook, I went back and update my master manuscript to fix them all. Recording the audiobook will help you find and fix any issues in your book including awkward phrasing, grammatical mistakes, missing words, or inconsistencies. In the end, that's a good thing! If you're recording someone else's audiobook, help out the author if you find obvious mistakes!

AUDIOBOOK TIPS AND TRICKS

Here are my top 5 audiobook creation suggestions to make the process smooth and fun rather than painful and frustrating:

- Monitor your recording. This means listening to yourself with plugged-in headphones while recording (a Bluetooth connection often creates a small lag causing an annoying echo). This helps you hear when you read something wrong or catch background noise getting picked up.
- Record the audiobook as soon as you publish the book so the content will be extremely familiar. It helps with the performance aspect of reading. Plus, you'll get more sales overall if it's available when the book launches. Some people *only* listen to books. Trust me, I hear this often!
- Drink water as you go. This helps you stay hydrated and prevents your voice from sounding dry. However, *never* drink carbonated beverages! I learned this lesson the hard way more than once… *burp!*
- Stay consistent in terms of your reading speed and distance from the microphone. This will simplify your editing and prevent having to rerecord sentences or sections.
- If you aren't technical at all or this sounds like too much work, you can hire a book narrator through ACX or Voices.com! You can also hire an audio technician to master the tracks. Obviously, there's a cost associated with all hires. With a narrator, you can agree upon a flat fee or offer to split royalties indefinitely. Expect to pay hundreds or possibly even thousands of dollars for any kind of help.

BECOME A NARRATOR!

Speaking of, you can earn money from narrating other people's books! You can earn passive income this route if you are able to agree to split royalties with the author. If it's a successful book, these royalties can certainly add up over time!

Sign up to be a narrator through ACX.com or Voices.com. It's a straightforward process. You sign up, fill out information about yourself, and submit audio samples. If you're a match in terms of what people need (think gender, age, and type of voice) you could get hired. Then it's microphone, no camera, *action*!

ALTERNATIVE WAYS TO EARN FROM AUDIO

Earning money from audio doesn't start and end with audiobook narration. Earning income from audio could be a great side hustle for you! Voices.com is a great resource to learn more and apply for gigs. You could offer your audio services for advertisements, online courses, video games, training videos, and many more voice opportunities. Even if you don't love your voice (most people don't!) there's somebody out there that could use your exact sound.

But never forget my personal rule #1: Always bring the enthusiasm! Even Idris Elba wouldn't land an audio role if he didn't put any effort into his performance! It's difficult to share tips for delivering a memorable performance but my best advice is:

- Try a section or chapter a few ways and listen back to it. Have a friend listen as well!
- Don't be afraid to speed up and slow down or add dramatic pauses.
- Be confident in being yourself.
- Picture sharing the story with a small audience if it's fiction or sitting down and speaking to one person for nonfiction.
- Stop recording when you recognize you're losing energy. Come back to the project with renewed energy another time!

MAY PASSIVE INCOME RESULTS (and a shameless plug...)

As I mentioned, my audiobook for *Save Half, Retire Fast* is available now, narrated by yours truly. I'm very proud of how it turned out. It's easily my best recording yet! In case you're wondering, I did make some sales! From the end of May through June I sold eight copies, earning around $40 in income. In Chapter 13 I'll update you on the performance of that audiobook. I also hope you'll consider giving it a listen when you finish this book. As a bonus, you might learn a thing (or 101!) about how to retire early! It's seven hours of my best personal finance content.

Find the audiobook on Amazon

FINAL THOUGHTS

Audio is an often overlooked opportunity for passive income but it could be your passive income unlock, especially if you take my advice to heart: Monitor your recording so you can hear yourself. Invest in quality recording equipment. Do all of your recordings in a day or on one weekend if possible for quality consistency. Keep chapstick and flat water nearby. Start with ACX (Audiobook Creation Exchange). It's the best place to publish audiobooks, especially for independent writers or beginners. And consider outsourcing post-production.

Finally, you can earn money with your voice beyond audiobooks with sites like Voices.com. Don't hesitate to think outside of the sound booth! Start a faceless YouTube channel. Start a podcast. Become a sound effects specialist. Give ASMR a shot! Find a site looking for voices to use as AI bots. If you have technical skills, become the person that edits and masters audio tracks instead of using your voice. Can you sing? Sing! The opportunities are out there! Can you *hear* them calling?

Questions for Reflection: *What feedback have you heard in the past about your voice? Does your voice motivate people? Does it put them to sleep? Do people enjoy your celebrity impersonations or silly stories? If you don't know, ask! Any feedback could be the information that helps you find your vocal niche.*

CHAPTER SIX
June: Low-Content Books

To do: Create a "to do" notebook

Have you ever wondered who makes the blank journal you use for notes? Or the calendar on the wall in your office? Or your grocery list pad magnetized to your fridge? Or empty sheet music a musician uses to create a song? Or even the guest books at a wedding? It turns out, anybody can!

These are considered "no-content" books or products. They're intentionally blank, or mostly blank, and ready to be used however the user wants to use them. You too can slap a trendy quote on the front of a blank notebook, find a print-on-demand service, list your product (with a description packed with popular search terms), and earn passive income from no-content books.

I had been learning and thinking about no-content books for years. I had the skills to create a handful for low to no cost. There's no inventory to keep. And I'm familiar with a great platform to use (Kindle Direct Publishing) so there's no learning curve or barrier to entry. I considered no-content books for my June challenge because it seemed relatively easy to pull off, which is key when you only have 30 days. But it didn't feel true to myself. Annoying inner-monologue guy spoke up once again when I veered off course. Sure, no-content books serve a purpose, but I'm an educator at heart. I loved the concept but I knew I could put my spin on it to help people even more.

I decided to create low-content books instead. Low-content books are books with minimal content or guided exercises. Some examples include a short guide with prompts, planners that include inspirational quotes on every page to reflect on, coloring books, gratitude journals, a meal-planning notebook, a book of word puzzles, and the list goes on. But are low-content books a realistic way to earn passive income? I was determined to find out. Here's what I learned and earned in June.

I bet you can tell which one I made...

MY LOW-CONTENT BOOK PASSIVE INCOME PLAN

In terms of revenue, don't get your expectations too high. I knew it's a volume play. Some people have published hundreds of no or low-content books, selling just a few copies a month. On the other hand, I know someone earning a thousand or more some months from selling them passively.

The first decision I needed to make was to set a goal for how many low-content books I wanted to create to sell in June. In research, I learned it can be very difficult to break through the noise and get noticed among all the competition on Amazon for low-content books. It's no longer a new concept ripe for early movers. I set a goal to create seven so I could play the volume game without over-committing myself. I was aiming for a balance of quality and quantity.

Next, I needed to decide on what types of books to make. Many creators recommended making content that's in line with your brand or other products such as supplemental material. With that in mind I reflected on supplemental material options for my three self-published personal finance books. My first two books contained 101 tips and challenges as the core structure. There's even a handy one-sheet checklist summary at the very end of each book. This gave me an idea: I could take the 101 tip list for each book and turn it into a companion notebook. This would give readers of the book a space to take notes, write down ideas, document their personal finance journey, and check off their accomplishments. (*As an aside, in hindsight I should have thought to make a brainstorm notebook for passive income ideas!*)

Pro tip: Make your title font large with contrasting colors to make it easy to read when it's a thumbnail.

BEAUTIFUL ON THE INSIDE...

To create the interior content for the books, I decided to put three of the 101 tips on each page with room to write below each tip. I mocked up a sketch of my notebook in a notebook (the irony isn't lost on me) and I drew consecutive lines to indicate the writing space for the user. I decided to add a blank notes page to the left of each page for extra writing space.

I used Canva to create the pages and I even took advantage of an offer to upgrade to Canva Pro at no charge for 30 days. This gave me more template options, one-click document resizing, and better export options that are great for printing. After a couple of hours of work, I had a completed 73-page document. It was relatively simple. I only had to make one page, duplicate it 34 times, and adjust the three tips on each by referencing them from my book. Then, I duplicated a blank page with the word "Additional Notes" on top 34 times and put these between my tips pages. Faster than it takes me to mow the lawn, my first low-content book interior was complete.

Once I made one of these 73-page notebooks, I was able to duplicate it all and quickly edit the 101 tips with minimal work to make the second notebook interior. Within three hours, I went from idea to two completed companion notebook interiors. Now I needed to give them a shiny coat of paint as a cover.

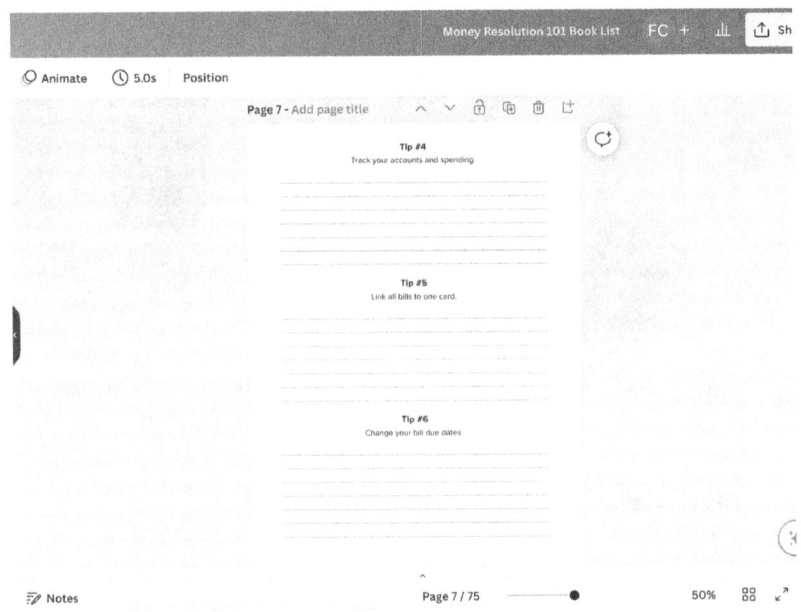

My simple "book" interior via Canva

AND BEAUTIFUL ON THE OUTSIDE!

There was still a major step in the process—I needed a compelling cover and a back-of-the-book design. I didn't want to spend money producing these books so I committed to making the covers myself, also in Canva. This part of the process was a little more challenging but still not too difficult.

While poking around my Canva account, I came across an old book cover template I designed in the past but never used. I knew it could work perfectly with a small handful of modifications and resizing. I wanted to give these low-content books a notebook feel so I changed the cover to white and added a little graph paper design in the background. *Note: Canva offers many book cover templates you can find and edit so you aren't starting from scratch.*

Before I made the cover, I needed to decide what size the books would be. I looked through the recommended size options in Kindle Direct Publishing and decided to go with 8.5" x 11". That's the size of printer paper and it would give the user a lot of room to write notes. (Looking back, I regret not choosing a smaller size. Most notebooks are roughly the same size as a paperback book.)

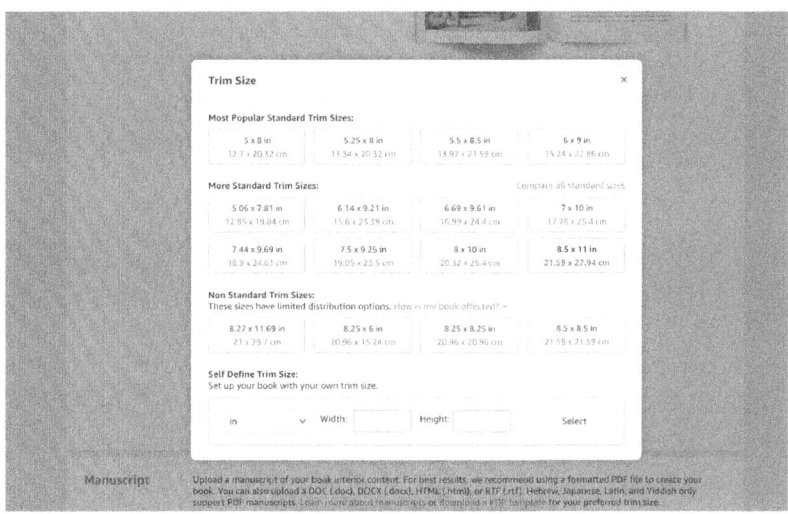

List of book size options available to self-published authors via Amazon Kindle Direct Publishing

Once done, I needed to resize my cover slightly to meet the exact requirement KDP provided—it needed to be a little larger than the book size to account for any minor discrepancies during the printing process. Then I quickly wrote a summary for the back of the book explaining what this notebook was for and how to use it. I also added a page of instructions for the first page of the book, so my notebooks were now 75 pages. I repeated the cover creation process for my second notebook and I was done.

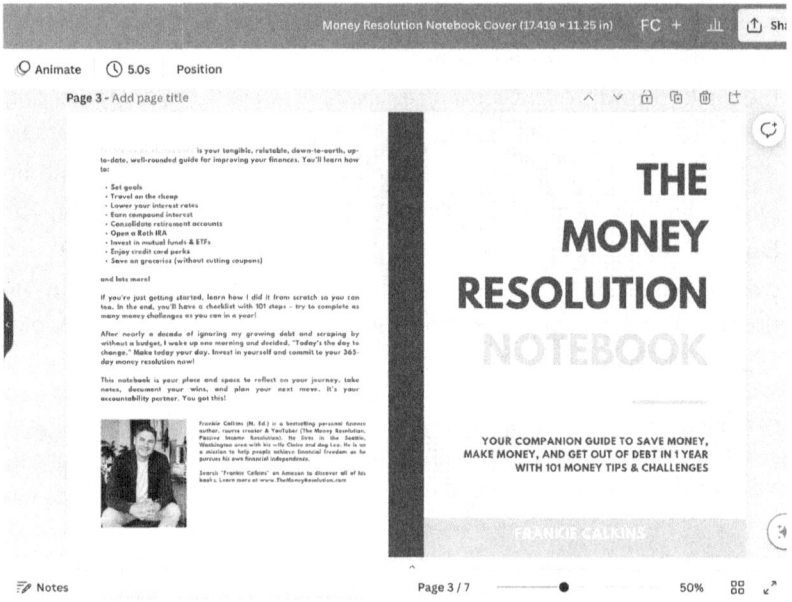

My final cover design in Canva

Both of my notebooks look similar overall with subtle nods to the main book on the front including the colors and font location. All told I spent around 3 hours making my first notebook. The second notebook took me less than 90 minutes of work to complete because I used the same Canva templates. To make my first book, I spent roughly an hour on the interior, an hour on the exterior, and an hour on the upload process within KDP. In four and a half hours, I created two low-content books and submitted them for review to be listed on Amazon. (In a moment, I will guide you through the entire creation and submission process.)

The third notebook I completed is a companion workbook for my online course Save Money Resolution. My course already included a

15-page PDF the user can fill out digitally. It's meant to be used as a workbook while taking the course. I thought there might be course takers who would be willing to pay a few dollars to have it all printed for them in a nice bound package.

Frankie Calkins

The author copy of my course workbook!

This book was only 35 pages—that's 15 pages of content, 15 blank pages for notes, plus an introduction and conclusion. I also included a blurb about how to save 25% on my course in the front that shows up on the Amazon "Look Inside" feature—which was intentional!

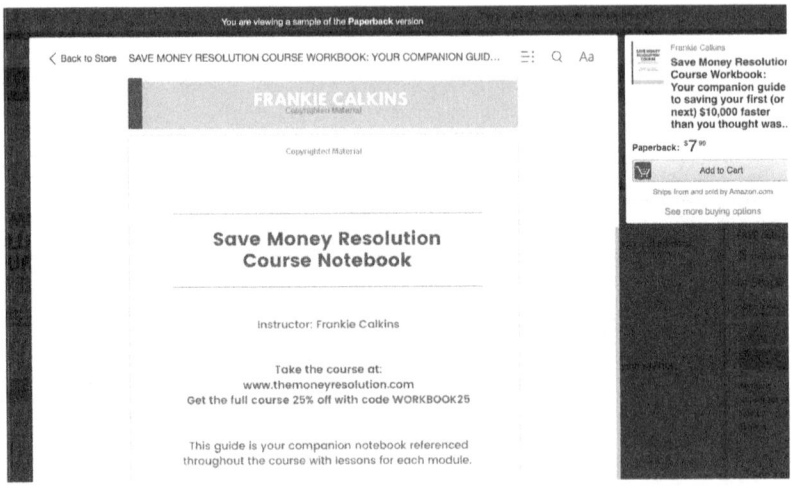

94

Pro tip: Put special offers in the front of your book so prospective buyers will see them in the preview on Amazon!

Overall, I'm super happy with how my books turned out. The quality was surprisingly great—it didn't feel cheap at all. I went with black ink on white pages and matte for the cover finish instead of glossy. Amazon does a great job with its Kindle Direct Publishing program. The cover colors look vibrant and the printing is fast!

The only downside is that printing costs for all books listed on KDP went up in mid-June 2023 which would decrease my royalties received for my low-content books. When I showed the workbook to my wife she was impressed, especially for something I pulled together in a few hours. She said it looked exactly like a workbook you'd get in school for a class or course. That's exactly what I was going for!

After these three low-content books I created four more to reach my goal by the end of the month. Here are the titles of those four books:

- Master Your Money in 30 Days
- 101 Things to Do in Early Retirement
- The Ultimate 3 Year Budget Planner and Tracker
- 101 Life-Changing Lessons About Money

Other ideas I considered include a password organizer, a vision board book, a passive income or side hustle income tracker, a bucket list notebook, and a student loan debt payoff tracker.

THE LOW-STRESS WAY TO MAKE A LOW-CONTENT BOOK

What else do you need to know to make a low-content book yourself? Here is a full step-by-step process in 3 parts: creating your book, publishing your book, and marketing your book. It's a more detailed summary of the process I went through. However, two chapters of this book are dedicated to marketing I'll gloss over part 3. You'll learn how to sell your books in Chapters 10 and 11.

I'll admit, this process is easier to show so I created a companion

45-minute full tutorial called *Low-Content Books Made Easy (with Chat GPT)*. It walks through this entire process with visuals and even more tips including how to use AI to speed a few steps up.

PART I. Creating Your Book

Perhaps nothing is more important than creating the right book for the right audience. Quality is crucial as well. These are the steps to work through to help your book stand out and attract the right audience on Amazon.

Step 1: Brainstorm Your Book Ideas

To create a successful low-content book, it's essential to understand your target audience and identify their needs. Here are tips for brainstorming a quality book idea that will attract eyeballs:

- **Research:** Explore popular niches on Amazon, via Google search, or even various online tools such as Jungle Scout to identify trends and popular themes. Look for underserved niches or gaps that you can fill with your ideas. The more you niche down, the better. Think about the exact words someone might search to find what you could create.
- **Consider Your Target Audience:** Determine who your book is for and what problems they might be facing. Think about your ideal reader's interests, hobbies, and goals, and brainstorm how you can help them overcome their challenges.
- **Generate Ideas:** Once you've identified your target audience and their needs, generate ideas that cater to those specific niches. Consider different formats, such as planners, journals, diaries, or notebooks. Think about the specific features and content that will resonate with your audience.

Step 2: Choose the Right Format

Now, it's time to choose the format that best suits your book and target audience. Here are some considerations:

- **Book Type:** Decide on the type of low-content book you want to create. It could be a guided journal, a daily planner, a recipe notebook, or even a combination of different types within a single book.
- **Size and Design:** Consider the size of your book and how it will be used by your audience. Will it be carried around or used at a desk? Think about the practicality of the size and the design elements that will appeal to your target audience.
- **Content Layout:** Plan the layout of your book's interior pages. Decide on the number of pages and whether you want to include prompts, templates, or empty spaces for your audience to fill in. Create a logical flow that guides readers through the book.

Step 3: Create and Format Your Low-Content Book

Once you have a clear vision for your low-content book, it's time to bring it to life! Here are the steps involved in creating and formatting your book:

- **Design the Book Cover:** A captivating cover is crucial for attracting buyers. Use design tools like Canva or hire a professional designer to create an eye-catching cover. Ensure it conveys the book's purpose and resonates with your target audience.
- **Develop the Book Interior:** Design your interior and format it as necessary for your book's purpose. You'll need to make decisions about the book's size (6x9 inches or 8.5x11 inches are common). You'll also need to think about a matte or glossy cover. From my experience, glossy covers print more vibrantly and look high quality.

PART II: Publishing Your Book

Let's discuss the important steps to prepare your low-content book for publication on Amazon through Kindle Direct Publishing (KDP). These steps ensure that your book meets the platform's guidelines and increases its chances of attracting readers and generating sales.

Step 1. Manuscript Preparation

Before you can publish your low-content book on KDP, you need to prepare your manuscript or interior. Here are some key considerations:

- **File Format:** Save your manuscript in PDF format. This ensures that the formatting, fonts, and layouts remain intact when viewed on different devices.
- **Page Numbers:** Add page numbers to your interior if desired. While low-content books don't typically have extensive text or chapters like a book, page numbers can still be useful for reference, organization, or finding a section.
- **Proofread and Edit:** Carefully proofread and edit your interior for any spelling, grammar, or formatting errors. Ensure the content is clear, concise, and free of any inconsistencies. It's smart to outsource this or at least ask a friend or family member to help you out!

Step 2. Create a KDP Account

If you don't already have one, create an account on Kindle Direct Publishing (KDP) at kdp.amazon.com. Sign in using your Amazon account or create a new one. Follow the prompts to set up your account, including providing bank and tax information so you can be paid!

Step 3. Set Up Your Book on KDP

Now it's time to set up your book on KDP. Here are some of the requirements you'll need to fill out:

- **Book Details:** Enter the required information, including the book's title, subtitle (if applicable, but recommended), author name, and series (if applicable). Write a compelling book description that accurately represents the content and appeals to your target audience.
- **ISBN:** Amazon no longer requires an ISBN (International Standard Book Number) for your low-content books. While it's not mandatory for KDP, having an ISBN can help with distribution and cataloging if you decide to provide your own via a local ISBN agency. It does cost money to request one and assign it to your book.
- **Keywords:** Choose relevant keywords that describe your book's content and target audience. These keywords will help readers discover your book when they search on Amazon. Try to think of keywords with high search volume but moderate competition. An AI resource like ChatGPT can provide keywords that are SEO-friendly to help your book with discoverability. You'll enter up to eight during the setup process.
- **Categories:** Select the appropriate categories and subcategories for your book. This helps Amazon place your book in relevant browsing lists and increases its visibility to potential readers.
- **Upload the Content:** Upload your prepared file (in PDF format) to KDP. Double check that the formatting and layout appear as intended.
- **Book Cover:** Upload your book cover. Make sure it meets KDP's requirements regarding size, resolution, and file format. Again, a high-quality cover is crucial. People absolutely do judge a book by its cover! *Note: You must have your full title on the cover.*

Step 4. Pricing and Royalties

Determine the pricing for your low-content book and set the

royalty options. Consider factors like printing costs, market competition, and your profit goals. KDP offers two royalty options: 35% royalty and the 70% royalty. The 70% option requires you to meet specific pricing criteria and includes distribution costs.

Step 5. Previewing Your Book

Before finalizing your book's publication, take advantage of KDP's preview tool. This allows you to review your book's appearance on different devices and identify any formatting or layout issues. Make necessary adjustments as you see fit. Approving the preview is a mandatory step in KDP.

Step 6. Publishing Your Book

Once you're satisfied with the book's preview, it's time to publish! Click the "Publish Your Kindle eBook (or Paperback)" button to make your low-content book available to readers on Amazon. Your book will typically be available on the site within 24 to 48 hours. Most of my books were approved and live on Amazon or available for preorder within 24 hours of submitting them.

PART III: Marketing Your Book

Congratulations on publishing your low-content book! However, the journey doesn't end there. To maximize its visibility and attract readers, you need to invest time and effort into marketing and promoting your book. Luckily, I'll cover effective free and paid marketing strategies in detail in Chapters 10 and 11! At a minimum, you can promote your book on social media and on your own author website. Plus, be sure to leverage the promotions and temporary discount features Amazon makes available to you if you make your book exclusive to Amazon.

Marketing and promotion require consistent effort and experimentation. Keep track of what strategies work best for your low-content book and adjust your approach accordingly. Double down on what works for future books and ditch the rest!

RESULTS AND FINAL THOUGHTS

As I mentioned, I did complete my goal of creating seven low-content books. They were all listed on the site by the end of June. That said, two weeks later, I was yet to record a single sale for these. However, at this point, I do recommend this side hustle because there are a ton of different no or low-content book ideas waiting to be made! You can also create a better version of something else that's popular. Not to mention, you can create and publish two or three in a single day if you're committed. It's low effort and potentially high reward. It's best for someone who's creative and has some basic SEO knowledge so you can stand out from the crowd and show up in search results.

Remember, the key to success lies in providing value to your readers. Focus on creating high-quality content, understanding your target audience's needs, and delivering on your book's promise.

Don't hesitate to embrace the power of automation using tools like ChatGPT to streamline your book creation process. AI can be a timesaver and game changer for you! Watch my full tutorial to learn more. I walk you through the entire process step by step, using ChatGPT to assist you along the way. From generating ideas and creating book layouts to optimizing your content and publishing on Amazon, my video tutorial will equip you with all the knowledge you need to create your own successful low-content book.

The low-content book market is not oversaturated. There's still plenty of time to get involved. Success comes to those who take action. So set yourself a goal and make one this week!

> *Questions for Reflection:* What types of no or low-content books or products do you currently use? What no or low-content books do you wish existed? What types of low-content books could you create? What are your creativity and creation strengths? What are your weaknesses you could outsource?

PART III

Third Quarter

CHAPTER SEVEN
July: Affiliate Marketing

How I partnered with 10 brands in 30 days as a small YouTuber

As a content creator, blogger, or anyone who runs a successful website, affiliate programs let you monetize the eyeballs you attract allowing you to earn a commission for promoting a product or brand. Done right, affiliate programs can be an excellent source of passive income. And people are figuring this out. Google Trends show that the search for 'affiliate program' and 'affiliate marketing' doubled between 2015 and 2021 and spiked in 2022.

Source: Google Trends

My challenge for July was to reach out to brands and get connected on affiliate platforms to give myself opportunities to promote products and earn passive income. In 2020, I earned my first dollar from affiliate partners so I went into my newest 30-day passive income challenge with a little experience under my belt.

With careful planning, persistence and a little luck, July was overall a success! In the end, I was able to partner with 10 brands. How did I do it? How can you do the same? Did I earn any income? Before we get to all of that, let's discuss exactly what affiliate marketing is because it can be a complex subject to explore if you're new to it.

AFFILIATE MARKETING EXPLAINED

In the past, referrals or "word of mouth" advertising helped businesses grow their brand and develop a loyal customer base. This type of marketing still exists but in the form of affiliate marketing. Users tend to trust the social accounts they follow. So, when an affiliate partner (aka a content creator, aka maybe you) promotes a link, the product or business they are promoting is generally seen as trustworthy.

In a nutshell it works like this: Jack follows famous person Jill on Instagram. Jill promotes a new solution for water in a bottle that doesn't require pails and wells. Jack buys the bottled water online to avoid having to fetch it himself up the hill, saving his crown in the process.

With affiliate marketing, brands pay their Jills (affiliates) based on performance—they don't pay affiliates unless the affiliate partners are able to sell products using their specific tracking URL. Generally, brands pay per sale on a set commission model called CPA (cost per acquisition). However, some may choose to pay their affiliates based on leads or link clicks via a CPC model (cost per click). Brands using a CPA model want to drive sales as the top priority. Brands using a CPC model are after eyeballs and brand recognition. Either way, affiliate marketing is a cost-effective way for brands to increase their sales, reach a new audience, and grow their business.

As you can imagine, this can be a complex marketing channel to organize and track for marketers so they rely on affiliate platforms. There are dozens of affiliate platform options for brands to choose which means there are dozens of platforms affiliate partners might need to know about or apply to use. This is where my research began. I researched to find the top affiliate platforms the top brands used. I quickly found that some are easy to join with a simple form but others require the user to fill out an application to prove they have a substantial enough following to be appealing for brands to connect with. If you don't have a large following or you get rejected, there is another way in the back door. You need to find a brand to partner with that sends you an invite to join.

THE NETWORK LANDSCAPE

The first thing I did was get re-familiar with affiliate partner networks I used in the past—some from personal partnerships and some from professional work experience as a marketer. Next, I moved onto researching the platforms I was less familiar with. Finally, I researched the ones I had never heard of. After a week of research my brain was nearly drained from the wave of information about dozens of affiliate programs I learned about. (*I wondered if Jill had a miracle water brand she recommended to fix that!*)

After pouring over dozens of articles and even researching the best products to promote, here are the 10 affiliate programs I found to be the most popular and most connected with top brands

- Impact
- Ascend
- Awin
- Commission Junction
- ShareASale
- FlexOffers
- AvantLink
- Clickbank
- Skimlinks
- GetResponse

Note: I wanted to add a sentence about each network to help you understand the differences but they are all very similar. Even multiple 'About Us' sections contained: "An affiliate marketing platform that empowers advertisers and publishers of all sizes to grow their business" and "Earn money by promoting the brands you love".

From my past partnership experience, I was already connected with Impact, Ascent, and Awin. Of the three, Impact was my personal favorite because it's easy to use and relatively easy to get connected with quality brands. In terms of the new affiliate program I learned about, I decided to apply to Commission Junction, Share-a-Sale, Flexoffers, and AvantLink. Their application process seemed easy to navigate and my likelihood of getting accepted felt stronger than the others.

The application process was unique for each platform. Generally, the platforms want to know how you plan to promote affiliate partner links. You also need to provide details about your website, social sites, how many followers you have, and more information that gives you legitimacy as a creator and influencer. Your job is to influence other people's purchasing decision after all! It's understandable that they only want to accept users who are serious about partnering with brands. You have to have a following of Jacks that know, like, and trust you and your recommendations.

At the time of applying in July 2023, I had 15,000 subscribers on my main YouTube channel The Money Resolution and 5,000 subscribers on Medium. I also had a 3,000 person email list I built by giving away free resources on my website. I didn't anticipate running into any roadblocks getting accepted.

Unfortunately, I was wrong.

My applications to join affiliate platforms were denied by Share-a-Sale and FlexOffers. Luckily, I was accepted by Commission Junction. My application stayed in pending status with AvantLink. I never heard back from them so I assumed that means I was rejected. No surprise—I learned only 30% of applications get accepted.

FINDING BRANDS TO PROMOTE

Next was the fun part: brainstorming brands I wanted to work with! When you promote products you use and like, it becomes easier to convince others to purchase your recommendations. I only wanted to promote brands I use and trust so naturally I made a list of all of the brands I use and trust!

At this point in July, I was on a "babymoon" with my wife in San Diego (*we found out we were expecting in late-February, which increased the difficulty level for all of my passive income challenges!*). She was lounging by the pool reading a book while I snuck away to the hot tub to do some brand brainstorming. I was shocked by how many brands I thought of. I quickly jotted down over 65 brands in the Notes app on my phone (my iPhone is "waterproof", don't worry!). It was going to require a lot of research to determine what, if any, affiliate platform they used to partner with people like me. So, the next morning, I grabbed my laptop and created a new tab in my Passive Income Resolution planning sheet and put each brand in 1 of 3 categories:

- Tier 1: Dream brands.
- Tier 2: Brands I use less frequently that I'd still support and trust.
- Tier 3: Brands that didn't fit with my channel or likely didn't have an affiliate program.

I challenge you to do the same; sit and reflect on brands you'd like to work with and promote in a perfect world. Seriously, it's fun!

Tier 1: Dream Partners	Tier 2: Next Best	Tier 3: Unlikely to Pursue
Apple	Prosper	Door Dash
Yeti	Rally	Epidemic sound
Nike	Udemy	Brooklinen
Unagi	Grammarly	Brads Deals
Honey	Bulletproof	Good Reads
Vint	Dodo Fetch	Fair Harbor
Canva	MoneyMade	Fundrise
Ally Bank	Kajabi	Marine Layer
Warby Parker	Discount Mags	BookBub
Dinnerly	Evo	Real simple mag
Alaska Airlines	Chase CC	Mainstreet
Fiverr	Spotify	JackThreads
Minted	Blue Nile	Nick Loper
Empower	Puffy Mattress	The Week
Shopify	Fandango	Ben Bridge
M1 Finance	Haven Life	PlayStation
Tesla	Google Domains	Redbox
Lulu Lemon	Fanatics	BLYT
Viori	Experian	Kindlepreneur
Vespa	DiscountMags	
Pawp	Redbox	
Costco	Evo	
Brooks	Haven Life	
MasterClass		

Go ahead, judge my life decisions…

Next, I researched each brand to see if they had an affiliate program and, if so, which affiliate platform they used. Roughly two out of three of my Tier 1 brands had an affiliate program and roughly half of my Tier 2 brands did. On a spreadsheet, I grouped brands together by affiliate platform:

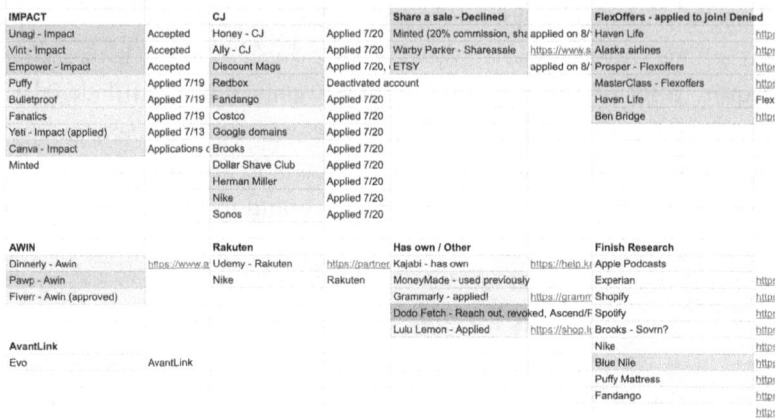

I highly recommend you document everything!

Note: Some brands have their own affiliate program and don't leverage the big affiliate programs. I decided not to pursue these brands because it was more hoops to jump through to apply and I wasn't qualified for most.

From there, it was time to apply to the brands that were using the affiliate platforms I was accepted into. Unfortunately, I had to eliminate 10 brands that were using affiliate platforms I wasn't accepted into. For the rest, I applied.

Each brand application was unique for the most part but the questions were often similar. I saved all of my answers to questions on the first few applications in a Google Doc so I could copy, paste, and edit my responses on future applications to speed up the process. It's worth it to take a few extra minutes to provide specific ways you'd like to promote each brands and why you'd like to work with them. Again, if they are brands you already know, like and trust, this should be easy! All told, I ended up applying to 26 brands I would be excited to

Passive Income Resolution

partner with and promote on YouTube and to my email list.

FRANKIE'S 5 STEPS TO PARTNERING WITH BRANDS

To summarize, my process for finding brands to work with was five steps:

1. Brainstorm a list of brands I already know, like, and trust.
2. Identify the top brands I want to work with the most.
3. Research each brand to see if they have an affiliate program.
4. Group brands together by affiliate platform (if applicable) and remove brands with no affiliate program.
5. Apply to be a partner with as many favorite brands as possible via affiliate platforms. *Optional: Appy to any top brands that don't use an affiliate platform directly.*

In the end, 10 of the 26 brands accepted me as an affiliate partner! By the end of July, I had 10 applications pending and I was rejected by 6 brands.

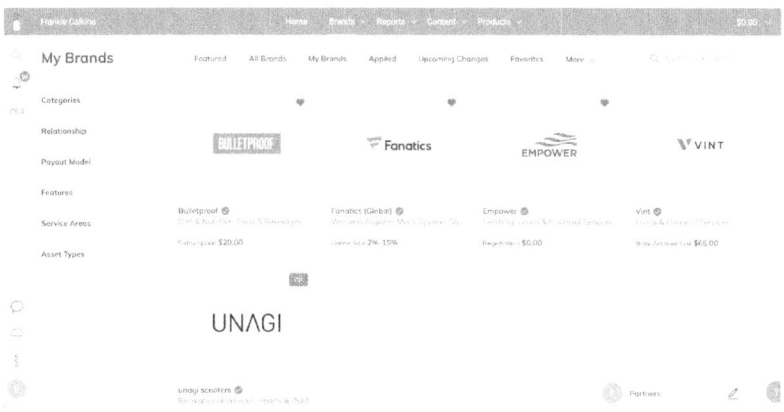

Advertiser Performance Today

Advertiser	Commission
Awin (USD)	USD 0.00
Fiverr Affiliates (Global Affiliate Program)	USD 0.00
Dinnerly (US)	USD 0.00
Motley Fool	USD 0.00
Tiller Money (US)	USD 0.00
Pawp (US)	USD 0.00

From	Subject
☐ Fandango	Sorry, your application was not approved
☐ DiscountMags.com	Sorry, your application was not approved
☐ NIKE	Sorry, your application was not approved
☐ Herman Miller	Sorry, your application was not approved
☐ Google Domains NA	Sorry, your application was not approved

A look at some of my brand partner acceptances and rejections.

SHOW ME THE MONEY!

So, how do you earn passive income from all of this? And is the income worth all the effort?

Your earnings from affiliate programs will depend on the commission model established by each brand. For example, the pay-per-sale model offers between 2% and 30% commissions on average while some companies offer flat commissions. The payment methods also differ. Some companies pay soon after a lead generation or sale. Others have a minimum threshold amount before paying out.

They're all unique so read through the information provided for each partner so you have a good understanding of potential income and payouts.

Of course, it's also up to *you* to figure out the best way to promote the brands to your audience. For me, that's highlighting brands as a sponsor of specific YouTube videos with a one minute mini-commercial in the middle of the video. I could also highlight brands as sponsors of broadcast emails to my list. For you, this might be promoting brand affiliate links within blog articles or on social media. Remember, users must click your personalized affiliate link in order for the brands to give you credit for the users that visit their website and make a purchase. The truth is, promoting the brands and convincing your audience to click on your partner links is arguably more difficult than connecting with brands in the first place—especially because I've guided you through the brand connection process! Unfortunately, I cannot show you exactly how to do that but, you certainly learn by doing and trying!

In the end, if you are successful in delivering eyeballs and sales for brands, the brands send money to the affiliate platform monthly based on performance and their outlined commission model. The platform pays you out. In most cases, the money is sent via direct deposit if you are willing to connect your bank with the platform.

FRANKIE'S 5 TIPS FOR AFFILIATE MARKETING SUCCESS

Here are a handful of my best tips I can offer if you're looking to get started with affiliate marketing.

1. Don't set your expectations too high.

When I first learned about affiliate partnerships and sponsorships a few years before this project I thought I would be able to unlock a massive passive income stream, even as a small YouTuber! I worked with five brands in the past and earned $1,500 total over a four year period. That said, I do still earn $20 to $50 most months from older videos that still successfully drive eyeballs to sites and help sell products (mainly my pet insurance videos). That payment is always a nice surprise and this is enough money to cover my pet insurance bill, for example!

2. Connect with brands and affiliate managers directly.

Try to get brand Affiliate Managers on a phone call or connect over Zoom. My most successful partnerships came after getting to know the people at the companies and talking through ideas to learn more about the brands and the best ways to promote them. A well-crafted direct email is a good way to start the conversation.

3. Keep your strategy simple.

Focus on cultivating really strong connections with a few brands you are most excited to work with. It is a lot less to manage compared to having 20 brands you are trying to promote across five different affiliate platforms. My approach isn't the method I'd recommend for most people. I was on a mission to learn and connect with as many brands very fast so I had more information to share with you but my energy was spread out, scattered and unfocused. Going forward, I already feel overwhelmed about the opportunities which can lead to analysis paralysis.

4. Don't include product promotions in every video, article, or social media post.

Promoting products and brands in all of your content can turn off viewers and subscribers. At a minimum, it will slow down the trust you need to establish with them as a priority first. I recommend promoting brands and products in roughly one out of every four videos or posts, depending on your niche and frequency of publishing. Remember, it's critical to build trust with your audience. Once they know, like and trust you, they will appreciate personal recommendations from someone they admire!

5. If you're a content creator, include your contact information in all of your videos or posts.

Do not use a personal email address for this. Create a new one for this purpose exclusively. I include my email address (frankie@themoneyresolution.com) everywhere—even now in this book! Most days I get a handful of partnership opportunities emailed to me. I'm uninterested in 99% of them but 1% of them do turn out to be financially beneficial. One emailed opportunity could change your financial life! Want to work with me? Send me an email with your idea! See what I did there?

JULY PASSIVE INCOME RESULTS

As I mentioned, I was able to successfully partner with 10 brands via multiple affiliate platforms. But, was I able to promote my links in July and ultimately earn any income?

Actually, *yes*! I worked with two brands on my new YouTube channel in July. The first was Vint, which is a company that allows users to invest in rare wines and spirits. You might remember I invested $100 into wine during my February alternative investing passive income challenge. In Chapter 2, I mentioned they were my first video sponsor as well! I made a dedicated review video in February about Vint because it's a company I use and trust after talking to the founder on the phone. I also featured Vint as a channel sponsor on a recent video with a 1-minute plug in the middle. From those two videos that included affiliate links in the description, I was able to drive 65 clicks from around 1,200 total video views. That led to 4 "actions" and $100 in revenue in just a few months.

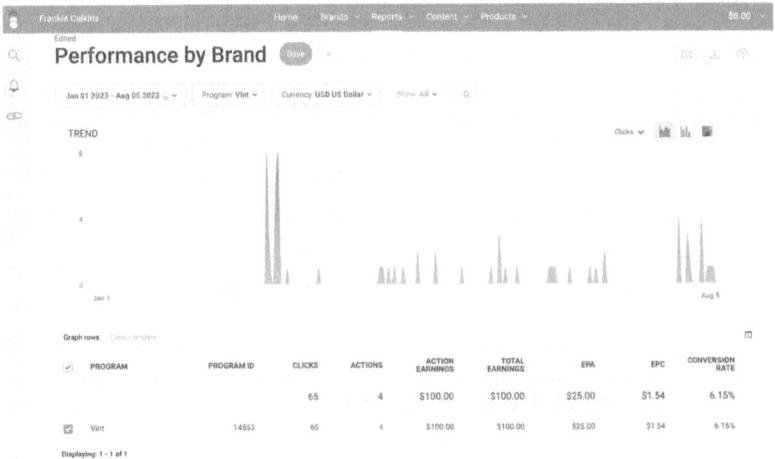

Author's Impact metrics. An "Action" was defined as an account creation and a bank account linked.

I was thrilled that my videos were able to convince four people to create a Vint account. Imagine if one of my videos went viral and ultimately earned 120,000 views instead of 1,200 views. At my current rate of one sign-up per 300 views, I'd get 400 users to sign up. If I earned $25 from each new user that signed up I would have earned $10,000 from one video!

If you'll allow me to fantasize for a moment, imagine if my Vint review video earned 1,000,000 views and my conversion rate held steady. In this scenario I would earn $83,333! *That's* the power of affiliate marketing!

Obviously, it's very difficult to create a 120,000 view video and conversion rates will vary. However, there are other routes to 120,000 views and $10,000 in affiliate revenue: You'd need to make 100 videos that earn 1,200 views each or 50 videos that earn 2,400 views each or 10 videos that earn 12,000 views each. None of these paths to $10,000 are easy by any means, but you can start to understand how affiliate marketing can be very profitable as it scales. To scale it, you have to show up consistently and put in the work. It pays off *literally* in the long run!

THIS CHAPTER IS SPONSORED BY...

Earlier this year, I received an email from another brand that offered an appealing partnership: Unagi. Unagi is an electric scooter company and they agreed to a channel partnership if I talk about my experience using their flagship scooter: the Model One Classic. They sent me a refurbished Model One Classic to use and keep in exchange for my honest thoughts during videos. They also provided me with a link to a Google Drive folder that had dozens of beautiful lifestyle photos and even videos that I could share with my users during the partnership segment. Here is the script I wrote and read during a video in July that featured Unagi as a sponsor:

Today's video is brought to you by Unagi Electric Scooters. I'm loving my Unagi scooter. It's one of the lightest electric scooters on the market at just 28 pounds, making it extremely easy to fold up and carry. It has 3 speed levels depending on your experience or preference and it maxes out at 20 miles per hour. Plus, you get up to 12 miles on a single charge or you could upgrade to the Voyager for up to 25 miles on a charge.

Not to mention, this thing is a looker! Both models come in 5 great color options. The Unagi scooter is well designed and looks and feels premium. It's crafted from high quality materials. And, of course, you'll save on gas. I use it to go to the gym or pick up groceries when I just need a few things. If I was still living in Seattle, I'd probably use it twice as much because parking and traffic are a nightmare in big cities.

If you're interested in buying, the Model one is under $1,000 but what's really cool is you can rent it for just $59 a month. Check it out if you could use some handy wheels and let Unagi know I sent you by using my affiliate link in the description. Thank you Unagi for sponsoring today's video. (My link: https://unagiscooters.sjv.io/6edxrN)

FINAL THOUGHTS

Affiliate marketing and promoting brands you love is an absolutely fantastic opportunity for content creators if you commit to it and can manage it. Of course, you also need to have an established audience, brands that align with your audience, and a strategy for promoting products or services.

Some content creators make the bulk of their income from affiliates, brand deals and sponsorships so it's great to learn about this path, even if you're small or just starting out. **It's a misconception that you need a lot of followers to work with brands.** I figured out how to find YouTube channel sponsors shortly after gaining 1,000 subscribers. A small, loyal following can be enough. Of course, a viral video or post helps as well!

The truth is, earning passive income from affiliate partnerships is 80% hard work and 20% luck. But you can create your own luck with dedication and perseverance! Finally, be true to yourself and authentic with your audience. They will see through bullshit. Never work with brands just for the money. Stick with brands and products you use and trust.

> *Questions for Reflection: Have you ever purchased a product that a friend or family recommended? How about an influencer? What are your tier 1, tier 2 and tier 3 brands that you'd love to partner with? If you have an audience, what types of products do you think they would like to hear about? If you don't have an audience, how could you start building one?*

CHAPTER EIGHT
August: Credit Cards

How to become a passive income pro with plastic

Can you earn a few hundred dollars a year in passive income from everyday spending by swiping your credit cards? If you do it right, absolutely! In fact, it might be the easiest passive income stream you're not thinking about. With the right strategies you might even earn $100 a month on autopilot as I do! This is the most set it and forget it passive income stream in this book. (*But **don't** forget to pay off your credit cards in full each month!*)

Ahead are actionable tips to help you make the most of your credit card usage. This chapter is perfect for passive income beginners but it's especially useful for anyone who has already dipped their toes into the credit card rewards waters and is ready to fully dive in. In the end, you'll be armed with the tips, skills and concepts that will excite you to take action immediately so you can start earning your first passive income dollars—if you haven't already. Specifically you'll learn:

- How to leverage sign-up bonuses
- How to master credit card point redemptions
- The secrets to maximizing cashback
- 10 of my favorite credit card tips and hacks
- What's in my wallet?
- What 2 new credit cards I added to my credit card portfolio this month and the full thought process behind it

3 WAYS TO EARN PASSIVE INCOME FROM CREDIT CARDS

As you likely know, you can use credit cards strategically to earn one time bonuses, points, rewards, or even cash directly in your pocket without changing your spending habits. I haven't swiped my debit card in over seven years. If you swipe yours more than once a week or even more than once a month, you're likely missing out on the easiest passive income source! Here are the three best ways you can earn passive income from credit cards you should be thinking about and planning for:

Earn Sign-up Bonuses

The easiest way to earn passive income from your credit cards is via sign-up bonuses. This is usually in the form of cashback or points in one lump sum once you hit the required spending in a specific time period.

That might require spending as little as $1,000 in the first 30 days on the credit card or as much as $10,000 in a six-month timeframe. Be sure you earn this offer if it's a compelling one. But do NOT spend money you wouldn't normally spend just to hit the bonus amount. Think about your spending habits and upcoming expenses before you sign up for a new card that has a sign-up bonus, especially if the required spending amount is high for your personal budget.

Master Point Redemption

Let's talk about earning and spending credit card points, because points and point structures can be intentionally confusing to prevent you from succeeding. Luckily, the same point structure is used for most cards that offer points for spending. Generally speaking, $1 spent will earn you 1 point. 100 points can usually be redeemed for $1. In some cases, points can be worth more, especially if redeemed correctly.

The devil is in the details so it's important to spend a little time learning about your card's specific point structure. If you're not sure where to find the information, browse through the login portal online. If you're still stumped, call the phone number on the back on the card and ask. Be sure to ask if points are worth more for different redemption categories. Then, use this knowledge to redeem points optimally for travel, gift cards, merchandise, cashback, or statement credit.

Again, your points can go further if you master how to redeem them. For example, in my Chase credit card portal, it explains that points can be redeemed 1.5 to 1 (100 points is worth $1.50) when used towards travel. But it's 1 to 1 (100 points is worth $1) when used for gift cards or cash back as a statement credit.

Master Cashback

Cashback rewards are exactly what they sound like: some money back in your pocket as a reward for using your credit card. You rarely see actual cash, but you earn money to spend as if it is cash. In some cases, cashback credit cards provide immediate value by reducing the amount of money you need to pay back on your card. In other cases, you might get a check in the mail or a gift certificate.

There are different types of cashback cards. The main two types are flat-rate and category-specific cashback cards. With a flat rate cashback credit card, you usually earn a set amount no matter the category of spending. A good example is the Citi Double Cash Back Credit Card where you earn 2% back on all purchases. With a category-specific credit card, you earn different percentages of cash depending on your category spending. This is outlined by each specific card. For example, the Blue Cash Everyday Credit Card from American Express gives you 3% back on groceries and gas and 1% back on everything else. *Note: All examples are as of August 2024. Rewards can and probably will change in future years.*

One unique card is the Citi Custom Cash Credit Card card which lets you earn 5% back on your top spending category and 1% back on everything else. The sneakiest cashback credit cards rotate their top categories every month. This requires more time and research so I would suggest you avoid these.

HOW TO BECOME A CREDIT CARD PASSIVE INCOME SAVANT

Here are my 10 best quick tips and hacks to help you master your credit card strategy to earn the most passive income:

1. Stack Your Plastic: Consider having multiple cards to maximize rewards across various categories. You can choose to keep it simple and have one to two good cards. But I encourage you to go beyond and spend time researching as I did in August to see if there are one or two better cards you can add to your credit card mix. Do this responsibly of course. I will detail my research and new cards in a moment.

2. Know Your Card Details: I have to reiterate this point—it's critical to know each card's reward type, spending category structure, and any other potential benefits. Document this and review this annually because it can change. In the beginning of August I took time to work through this exercise for all of my current cards (more to come about these).

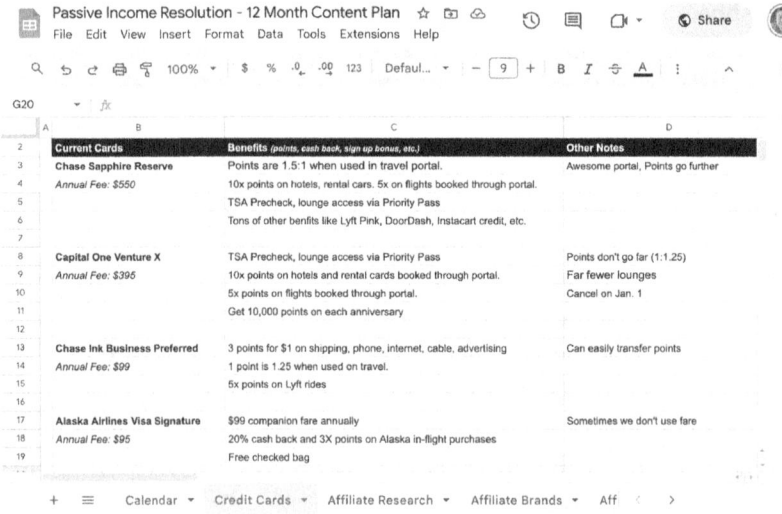

Get full access to my passive income master planning document for free at https://bit.ly/passiveincomesheet

3. Use the Right Card: Use specific cards for specific spending categories to earn higher rewards. Using your card knowledge you can make sure you're using each card for the right spending to optimize your earning. There are ways you can ensure you do this. For example, keep your gas card in your car or only save one card in your Amazon account.

4. Pay Cards in Full: This is credit card 101. You must avoid interest charges by paying off your balance in full each month. Interest and late payment fees can wipe out any earnings, making this passive income opportunity a complete waste of your time. In the worse case scenario, you pay more in interest and fees than you earn each year. This is how credit card companies win.

5. Redeem Wisely: Choose redemption options that offer the highest value per point or dollar. The example I shared earlier was my Chase Ultimate Rewards points go further when redeemed for travel. Alternatively, I get 80 cents on the dollar if I were to use Chase points at checkout on Amazon.

6. Referral Bonuses: Many cards offer a one time bonus if you refer a friend or family member to sign up for their credit card. This is a simple strategy that many people often forget about, even when they suggest specific cards to friends and family! They must use your specific personal URL or code when signing up, which you can likely find in your credit card portal.

7. Annual Fees: Some cards require you to pay a one time fee each year just for having access to the card. Evaluate whether the rewards more than justify any annual fees your cards have. Cards with higher fees often offer better rewards and even perks (for example: lounge access at airports and TSA precheck). But if you don't spend the card correctly, redeem points smartly, or take advantage of the perks, a high-fee card won't be worth it. Some fees can be as high as $695 or more and annual fees can increase annually. However, there are dozens of fantastic cards with zero annual fees. I'll share two I love in a moment!

8. Keep Accounts Active: Regularly use your cards to prevent points from expiring. For some cards, points might expire after 5 years or you lose them all if your card gets closed due to inactivity. Don't let this happen! A closed credit card will also likely have an impact on your personal credit score.

9. Utilize Online Portals: I keep referring to online portals and here's another reason to use them: some credit card companies offer extra rewards for shopping through their online portals. Chase has an excellent online portal. It's easy to navigate and offers great rewards and perks that are clearly outlined. However, Capital One's portal has room to improve. There are no extra perks for using the portal and the portal always takes forever to load pages!

10. Don't change your spending! This point is critical. Do not use cashback, points, or perks as a reason to spend more money. Don't let welcome bonuses turn into shiny object syndrome that prevent you from reading the potential new credit card's interest rates, fees, and other details. Use credit cards responsibly and always avoid overspending for the sake of rewards.

WHAT'S IN MY WALLET?

Here are the credit cards I've used for years, the card I decided to close after research, and the new credit cards I added in August for passive income—that won't change my spending habits.

Credit Card #1

My go-to primary card is the Chase Sapphire Reserve. This is a very expensive card so I only recommend it if you're going to take full advantage of the benefits. The annual fee is $550 a year but it has loads of benefits such as TSA precheck, monthly DoorDash credit, Priority Pass lounge access at airports, a Lyft membership, and more.

I also redeem $300 a year in travel credit (redeemable if I book at least $300 in travel each year in the portal). This effectively reduces the annual fee to $250 a year. For many, that is still an uncomfortable amount. Personally, I usually earn around 30,000 points a year from normal spending. Those points are redeemable for $450 if used on travel in the Chase portal. I typically cash in at least that amount every year for vacation. That's a net profit of $200 annually, plus the aforementioned perks I often use.

All of this is to say, I love to travel but I do get stressed out about the cost to do so and the airport process. This credit card helps alleviate both of those stressors!

Credit Card #2

The credit card I used the next most often is one I paired with my Reserve—the Chase Ink Business Preferred. This card is used to get me 3x points back on most expenses related to my business such as cable and cell phone bills. It carries a $99 annual fee. The reason I chose this business card is because I love how easily I can transfer points from this card to my Reserve card. Therefore I maximize the amount of points I earn in business categories and I use them effectively to add to my travel points that are worth $1.50 per 100 points.

Between these two cards, I've redeemed 138,000 points in the last 18 months which was worth close to $2,000 between travel bookings and the pay-yourself-back feature. This is unusual but we took two trips in 2023. Over half of our airfare, lodging, and transportation were covered by points which I earned passively! We also don't typically use the pay yourself back feature but 2023 also included several unexpected house expenses we chose to charge so we took advantage of that as well.

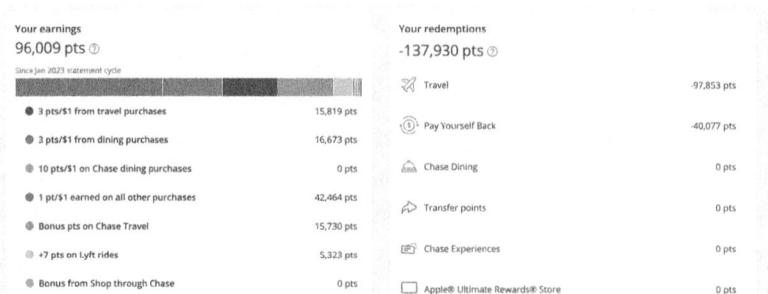

Author's Chase portal summary of the previous 18 months.

You're Outta Here!

The credit card I regret that I closed in August was the Capital One Venture X card. This card had a very attractive sign-up points bonus at the time that I couldn't resist (100,000 points!) but the points don't go nearly as far as Chase points when redeemed. You get $1 for 100 points for all types of ways you can redeem them. Plus, several of the benefits overlap with my Reserve card because it's also a travel focused credit card. None of this would be a total deal breaker without an annual fee but that is also high at $395 a year. I cannot recommend this credit card. I fell victim to "shiny object syndrome" and learned this lesson the hard way!

New Credit Card #1

Most of my current cards are focused on travel cards so I decided to dip my toes into the cashback waters. It didn't take me long to identify two easy wins for myself and my family. Both of the cards I added this month are no-fee cards, which was non-negotiable for me. Both are store-specific because I don't want to have to think about categories and cards when spending on the go.

First, I signed up for the Costco Anywhere Visa Card by Citi. Since buying our first house almost 2 years ago, our Costco spending has doubled. We've had a few big purchases such as new blinds. We also have more bathrooms, a yard to care for, a bigger pantry to keep stocked, and more rooms to clean. Plus, we have a new family member on the way!

List of Costco Citi credit card benefits

With this card I get 2% back on all purchases in addition to the 2% back I already get as an Executive Member. That's 4% back on all Costco purchases. Plus, it's a rare card that earns you 5% back on EV charging and we own an electric vehicle so that bonus will come in handy.

After doing some research, I determined we spent $7,650 at Costco the prior year. We earned roughly 7,650 Chase points from that spending which equated to around $100 in travel redemption cash. With the Costco card I would have earned $153! The only drawback: Costco cashback arrives annually in the mail in the form of a gift certificate you have to use at Costco. We are okay with this because we make a monthly trip to Costco already. This credit card won't change our spending habits and it keeps things simple: *only* use this card on Costco purchases!

Net Annual Earnings: $53 more than using our Reserve card at Costco.

New Credit Card #2

There is one other place we spend a lot of money (and we're probably not alone): Amazon. Again, with a newborn on the way, we expect to spend even more at Amazon over the next few years. After research, we decided the Amazon Prime Visa credit card made a lot of sense for us. We get a whopping 5% back on Amazon purchases in the form of Amazon credit that gets added to our account each month automatically.

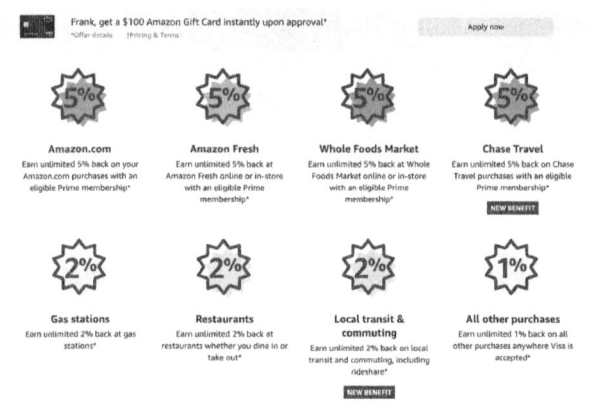

List of Amazon credit card benefits

Looking back at the last year we spent $2,340 at Amazon. We earned 2,340 Chase points worth around $30. With the Amazon card, we would have earned $117 in cashback the easy, automatic way.

Net Annual Earnings: $87 more than using our Reserve card at Costco.

With these two cards, we are set to earn an additional $140 in passive income from everyday spending every year. I expect this number to be closer to $200 with a newborn. Our electric vehicle is relatively new to us but that Costco credit card perk could increase this amount even more. We also received a one-time $100 Amazon gift card bonus for opening up this new credit card.

$200 annually may not be a large sum of money for some, but it's essentially free money after doing some research and adding these two cards to our credit card mix. Add that to the $395 we'll be saving from cancelling our Capital One Venture X card and $600 a year suddenly does make a big difference on our bottom line! Over 10 years, that would equate to a minimum of $6,000 in "free" passive income.

FINAL THOUGHTS

If you are thinking about a cashback card, don't settle for less than 4% back on your top stores or spending categories. For example, you might want to consider the Citi Custom Cash Card. It's a flexible card allowing you to pick which category earns you 5% back in cash. For me, I would use that towards groceries. I'll probably research the best card specifically for groceries in the near future!

If your credit card mix gets complicated because you have to use different cards for many different categories and use cases, literally label your credit cards so you know which to use when you're on the go. You can do this with tape and a marker or a label machine!

Finally, I challenge you to do what I did the last 30 days as a challenge. Review your spending. Review your credit cards and current benefits. Determine if you need to change which card you use per category, cancel cards, or add new credit cards to your wallet. Perhaps you too can earn hundreds or even thousands a year in passive income as I have in point redemptions.

(I'd be remiss if I didn't mention there is a group of people who love "credit card churning". In simple terms, think of it as doing what I did this month every month. For people who do this, credit card churning is a passion and a hobby. To learn more, there is a subreddit community you can explore at reddit.com/r/churning. If this sounds interesting, proceed cautiously for reasons I've already shared!)

With careful planning, credit cards can be a valuable tool for financial growth and passive income. But never forget, adding and removing credit cards will have an impact on your credit score. I recommend you track your credit for free as I do with Experian. Skip the paid plan when you sign up and you can still track your score.

And never forget: always pay off your credit cards in full each month. Otherwise, come back to this chapter when you are in a position to do so!

Questions for Reflection: *Do you know your credit score? What percent of the time do you use your debit card or cash vs. your credit cards? Do you know how much you pay in credit card annual fees? Do you know your top spending categories? Be honest, did you think credit cards were a reliable source of passive income before you started this chapter? I hope this chapter alone more than pays for your book purchase!*

CHAPTER NINE
September: Self-Publishing

"If there's a book that you want to read, but it hasn't been written yet, then you must write it." -Toni Morrison

Welcome to the meta chapter where I share all about attempting to self-publish my 4th book (in 30 days or less) in the middle of my 5th book.

Some people take years to write a book. However, with experience under my belt and a fire lit under my *you-know-what*, I felt confident I had a quality book I could create and share with the world in less than a month. Yes, it would be very difficult. But I was motivated, especially by my self-imposed deadline. Plus, I craved that incredible sense of accomplishment and self-satisfaction you feel on "pub day" (the day your book is published). The pub day feels are addictive! Could seeking those good vibes alone push me enough to create such a difficult passive income stream in a month? Probably not. I needed a book I was excited to write.

Lucky for me, I wasn't technically starting from scratch. I had an idea and progress in motion. I had been working on a book for the previous year and a half without even realizing it. After years of studying the how-to of personal finance, I spent some of 2021 and all of 2022 diving deep into the world of finance psychology. The book concept and outline was right under my nose. This book would become the inevitable child created from all of the content I had been making and sharing online in recent years.

I knew from my mindset research the last year and a half you can achieve anything you set your mind to with the right attitude. That would be the theme of my book and it was this same mindset that led me to believed I could write a full-length book in less than a month. Everything I had learned and done recently was for this moment. All that was left was to roll up my sleeves and do the work. I wanted to write this book. I needed to write this book. Now was my chance to commit to it.

Here's a little bit more about how I got to this moment, exactly how I tackled such a daunting task, and exactly how you can do the same.

PROJECT MINDSET

Two years ago I published my 3rd book "Save Half, Retire Fast". Immediately after I knew the concept of my 4th book would be focused on developing a strong money mindset (I'll admit, I was getting burnt out on how-to money topics and the book "The Psychology of Money" really inspired me!) I wanted to continue to make videos weekly on my first YouTube channel "The Money Resolution" so I committed to shifting from early retirement videos to videos about developing a strong money mindset throughout 2022. I had a feeling these videos wouldn't perform as well as my "save half" videos but that wasn't important to me. As a creator, there are times where you need to follow your heart for your own happiness. This was one of those moment.

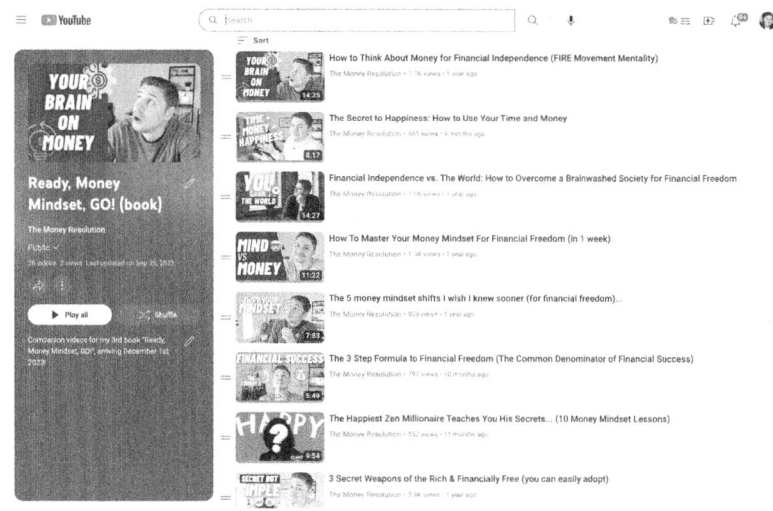

My Money Mindset video playlist

Per my usual routine, I repurposed those video scripts into articles I eventually posted on the site Medium. I always spend a lot of time publishing those articles *just in case* they end up becoming a chapter in a book one day. It was finally time to return to those articles and create a book out of them.

The hardest part was done; a good chunk of the content was written. Now it was a matter of finding the best content from my 50 or so articles and putting them together in an order that makes sense and pulls the reader along an inspiring journey. Then of course edit, edit some more, edit some more, format the e-book, make a book cover, write blurbs, edit some more, format the paperback, upload to Amazon, and wait to hopefully get approved while stressing about minor typos that always slip through, marketing, sales numbers, and public reception. No sweat right?

Here's a realistic, less dramatic guide to self-publishing and how I tackled each step in September.

FRANKIE'S SELF-PUBLISHING GUIDE

There were 7 critical steps (or tasks) I knew I needed to accomplish to create the book:

1. Create a compelling book title and subtitle
2. Outline and write the chapter content
3. Organize the content to ensure it flows
4. Edit, edit, and edit some more!
5. Format and export the manuscript
6. Create a book cover and write a compelling book description
7. Upload to Amazon KDP in multiple formats

For the most part, I completed these steps in order but there was plenty of overlap and back and forth between steps. You could tackle these steps in a different order but this was, and has been, my project method historically.

Completing these steps are universally required, regardless of your preferred order or how quickly you're hoping to publish your book. Obviously, how to write and self-publish a book could be it's own book (many already exist!) but here are my step-by-step highlights followed by my best advice.

Step 1. Create a compelling book title and subtitle

At some point while making my money mindset videos and articles throughout 2022 I created a note in my phone titled "Book 4: Money Mindset". In it, I jotted down ideas and notes that came to me randomly. I also wrote down title ideas. Before starting the book process, I first reflected on those titles. For some reason, having a great title is something that excites and motivates me. When I know my title, it's as if I can already picture holding the finished product in my hands! It becomes my north star in a sense.

I browsed my rather generic list of title ideas. A few gave me a chuckle. I added a handful of new ideas during a quick brainstorm. When nothing immediately stuck, I tried to leverage Chat GPT. It wasn't helpful. I didn't think there was an audience for "The Positive Money Paradigm: How to Elevate Your Prosperity Consciousness".

Ultimately, the most helpful exercise was reading my two dozen title ideas out loud to my wife. She hardly had to give feedback or react. I knew almost instantly which titles to cut and which titles were the finalists (there's something about an audience that helps you realize what works and what doesn't). A few minutes later I knew my title. It was in my gut all along but I needed help processing my thoughts out loud. I also wrote a dozen subtitles but put a pin in that exercise until later.

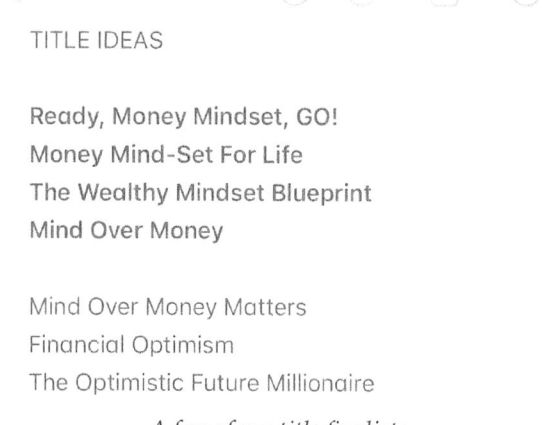

A few of my title finalists

Step 2: Outline and create the content

If you're writing a book from scratch, outlining your content is a critical step you shouldn't be in a hurry to complete. It's the backbone, the structure, that keeps the book on track and keeps you focused as you write.

I started working through the book content by making a spreadsheet. On it I wrote down the Medium article titles related to the topic money mindset. I added a link to each article so I could access them quickly. Then I painstakingly read all 44 articles, many of them twice, over the course of a few days. I scored each article out of 10 on a very subjective personal scale and added comments about how they would or wouldn't fit into the book. I also noted any additional work that was needed for polish.

Rank	Title	Link	Notes
6	25 Mini-Money Mindset Lessons	LINK	Move towards end or cut? Tip #
6	3 Most Important Words in Personal Finance	LINK	Very similar to anti-budget article
10	3 Secret Weapons of the Financially Free	LINK	Great chapter. Hits 3 main point
7	Being the Boss of Your Money (Pay Yourself First)	LINK	Pay yourself first - merges how
10	Common Denominator of Financial Success	LINK	Inspired writing. Very few edits
5	Common Paths to Early Retirement	LINK	Still need to edit. Most of these
9	FI Isn't for the Rich, It's for You: How to Redesign Your L	LINK	Good articles reinforcing a lot of
6	Fighting Financial Monsters	LINK	First half is a little long and tone
7	Financial Cheat Days	LINK	Good, original concept about the
7	Financial Freedom Bucket List	LINK	Good concept but needs some
10	Financial Freedom vs. The World	LINK	Excellent first chapter. About ov
6	Fire vs. FOMO	LINK	Direct and easy to follow but FC
5	Habits of the Perpetually Broke	LINK	Still need to edit. Most of these
8	Hidden Reasons You Can't Save Money	LINK	Introduction needs some work.
4	How Ordinary People Retire Early	LINK	Did not edit. Too much strategy.
9	How to Make Financial Freedom a Priority	LINK	Great article with 9 steps. Well

My first pass via my planning document. Get access to this and more at https://bit.ly/passiveincomesheet

Step 3: Organize the content to ensure it flows

Organizing the content for flow was an exciting step because it was the moment the book started to come together. For starters, I sorted the content scores from best to worst. I decided to remove anything that was a 5 or less. Next, I grouped them together via themes that would make up the different parts of the book. Within those parts, I organized the articles (AKA chapters) in an order that I felt flowed best. This took a few hours but, once done, I committed to it. I didn't want to continue to waver on what to include or not include or agonize over the order. My 30-day timeline wouldn't allow for it!

"Don't be afraid to kill your darlings" was a phrase kicking around in my head as I went looking for articles to remove. I wanted to include them all. They're all my babies! But I made a rule to cut out roughly half. Each article was a *"Hell, yes!"*, or it was a no. I even cut three articles I rated a 7/10! I considered a 7 a "good" score, but only "great" or "outstanding" or "best-in-class" would make the cut!

Steps 2 and 3 should take a great deal of time to complete if you're starting this process with nothing written. For many, finishing a completed manuscript takes months or even years! If you don't have articles ready to plug and play as chapters, think of each chapter you write as an article (or even blog post) rather than a very small part of a potentially long book. Don't think ahead about how much you haven't written—that will feel overwhelming and you'll want to give up. Focus on completing one chapter at a time, or even sections of a chapter, as you write. Before you know it, you'll be over halfway done! Then, the second half becomes much easier as you can actually start to see the light at the end of the writing tunnel.

	MENTALITY VS. REALITY (7)		Notes
10	Financial Freedom vs. The World	LINK	Excellent first chapter. About overcoming a brainwash
10	How to Think About Money for Financial Success	LINK	Or this could be the first chapter... little edits needed
9	Money and Manifesting for Beginners	LINK	So far these chapters feel in the right order. Or swap
7	Time vs. Money vs. Happiness	LINK	"The Formula for Happiness". Needs some editing, e:
7	The 7 Personalities of Money	LINK	Reads a little like horoscopes. Fits in book I think. No
6	5 Mini-Money Mindset Lessons	LINK	Move towards end or cut? Tip #4 feels out of place a
6	Sticks vs. Carrots	LINK	Move towards end or cut? Concept might contradict t
	A RICH LIFE (5)		
10	The Happiest Millionaire's Mindset Secrets	LINK	Great start to this section. Reinforces lots of previous
10	Common Denominator of Financial Success	LINK	Inspired writing. Very few edits needed. Motivating ye
10	3 Secret Weapons of the Financially Free	LINK	Great chapter. Hits 3 main points and ties them toget
8	Real Wealth Has Nothing to Do With Money	LINK	Moved fisherman story to front. It's personal but that's
9	FI Isn't for the Rich, It's for You: How to Redesign Your L	LINK	Good articles reinforcing a lot of prior concepts. Patie
	OVERCOMING FINANCIAL CHALLENGES (6)		
7	The Seduction of Pessimism	LINK	Introduction needs a little work. Takes a while to get i
6	Fighting Financial Monsters	LINK	First half is a little long and tone is different. Big focus
6	Fire vs. FOMO	LINK	Direct and easy to follow but FOMO as a big topic do
7	Overcoming Financial Hardships Big and Small	LINK	Mostly about my story and crisis but emotional, perso
7	Overcoming Mental Roadblocks for Financial Freedom	LINK	Has 8 sections in total. Could probably cut it down to

My organized book sections and chapters

Step 4: Edit, edit, and edit some more!

I will admit, editing is my least favorite part of the book creation process. It's also arguably the most important part. Errors are distracting. And you wouldn't have great movies without great editors! (*This is also me reminding myself to focus and stay motivated as I work through editing this book in your hands!*) If you decide to spend money on your book creation, I highly recommend you invest in a quality editor or editors. I didn't have the budget for one so I got creative and found editors via $7 Craigslist ads in the past. You can also hire editors from the site Fiverr—though you get what you pay on sites like these. Worse-case, you can enlist family and friends you trust to help you out. Best-case scenario, one of your friends or family members are also a writer and you can exchange editing services for free!

I've tried all of those options in the past but I was determined to create this book 100% on my own for the sake of time so I took on the editing myself. Luckily, I spent a good deal of time editing these "chapters" when I turned my videos into articles. I found minimal line edits were needed and there were only a handful of pesky typos to fix. I did need to improve my introductions and add a transition from one chapter to the next to help improve the flow where possible.

I told myself it's okay if my book contains a few errors or mistakes in the end. I'm only human and I'm doing this challenge alone intentionally for the sake of time. Plus, I can always fix issue after publishing—that's the beauty of self-publishing on Amazon! You could also use ChatGPT or Grammarly to clean up your chapters (there's no shame in using available AI tools). However, if you rely on AI too much, I found it often strips out human personality and your voice. My voice in my books is extremely important to me! It's uniquely me. You are uniquely *you*!

Step 5: Format and export required files

Formatting can also be tedious and time consuming because it requires technical skills. You might be intimidated by the thought of formatting your book but I recommend you consider formatting yourself. Yes, it can be frustrating at first. But, in my experience, I found it's far more frustrating to rely on somebody else and it can be pricey. I paid someone on Fiverr to format my first book and it took weeks and dozens of rounds of requested changes. He would fix one formatting mistake, only to introduce a new one!

I learned to format for my second book and now I have the skillset so I can adjust issues easily and save money and time while I'm at it. I've always used the program Scrivener to format my books. For exporting, I focused on creating my ebook first which required an ePub file. I used a free Kindle Previewer app to review the file. Then I exported a PDF version for the paperback. It took me less than an hour to adjust the ebook formatting to paperback formatting. I highly recommend you launch your book with both options for the reader!

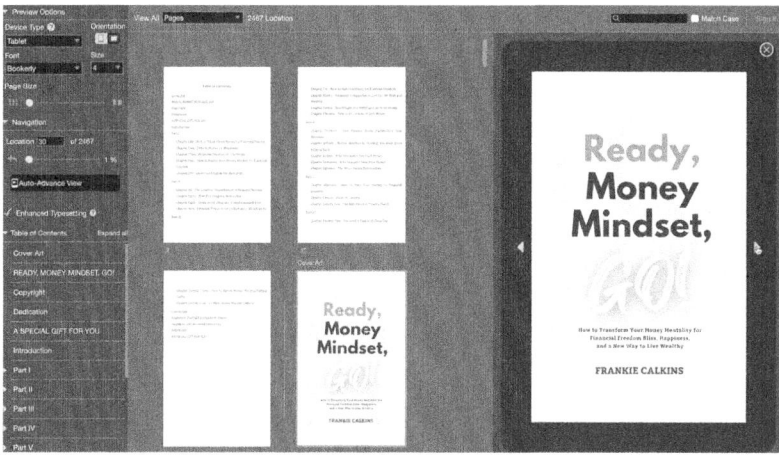

Get this ebook Preview program free from Amazon KDP

It takes a lot of tinkering with export settings to get everything just right but it feels amazing when you finally see your completed book in full in digital form. I'm always most excited to find out the page count. My page count upon export when finished was 217!

Note: You can create an ebook of any length. Some readers prefer a short book that can read in one sitting!

Step 6: Create a book cover and book description

This was also the first time I decided to take on the book cover design, mainly due to timing. Typically, the back-and-forth process with a designer can take a month or more. I was on a self-imposed 30-day deadline so I gave it my best shot, leveraging my experience making several covers via Canva from my low-content book challenge earlier in the year. I tinkered with ideas in Canva and after a few hours, I had a cover I was happy with.

When I ordered my author copy, I noticed a few changes that were needed, but I still liked it very much overall. The white background represented a clean slate or fresh start for the reader. It felt approachable and optimistic. It felt fresh and optimistic compared to the dark grays and blacks of my previous books. I also tried to use colors that would appeal to all genders. Here is how the final cover turned out:

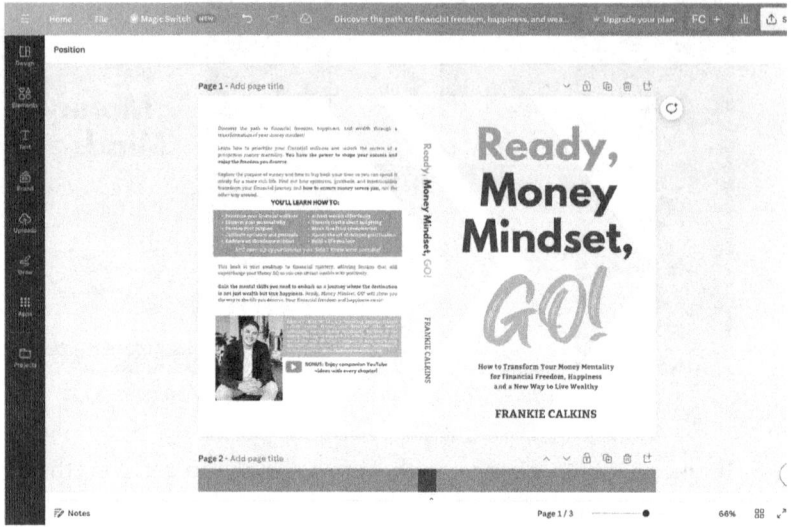

Updated book cover design after ordering my author copy

My final version was even more minimal than the original. I also updated it from a matte finish to a glossy finish, which made the colors print more vibrantly. It took about an hour to write and edit the book description for the back of the paperback cover, leveraging past templates from my previous books. I used a slightly longer version of this description for my Amazon book description. Speaking of Amazon…

Step 7: Upload to Amazon Kindle Direct Publishing

This step can be an hour or less if you have done it before but might take a few hours or a few days if you're uploading a book for the first time. In short, you enter the book details, upload the content, and approve the layout. Then you set your available regions and pricing. You'll need to make key decisions along the way such as your book categories, book keywords, whether to make it exclusive to Amazon, whether to use your own ISBN, and more. Years ago I made a step-by-step tutorial you can watch on YouTube called "How to Self-Publish a Book on Amazon in 30 Days" on The Money Resolution YouTube channel.

SUMMARY

Those seven steps probably sound like a lot to accomplish, especially in 30 days (*especially* if you have a full-time job as I do). There's a reason very few people write a book in their lifetime! Don't be in a hurry. A quality book is the goal. Perfection is not. Don't let perfection be the enemy of good.

Consider creating your book the way I did by writing articles and turning those into chapters. Alternatively, you can do it the other way I've done it in the past: outline the book, outline the chapters, then write a chapter at a time. From there, if you desire, you could turn those chapters into YouTube videos and articles to repurpose content the other way around!

10 TIPS FOR FIRST-TIME AUTHORS

This is the 4th time I've gone through the entire process (5th if you count this book) so I've learned a lesson or two or 100! Here are my personal top 10 tips any first-time author needs to know—some of which will be repeated because it's important:

1. Publish with Amazon KDP only. It might sound exciting to find an agent and a publisher to get behind your book but it's a very difficult process (trust me, I tried very hard for this book!). Make your self-published book exclusive to Amazon KDP because it's fast, efficient, and relatively easy. Plus, there's already a huge audience—Amazon started as a book company after all! Not to mention, they offer marketing and promotional benefits if you make your book exclusive to Amazon. Ingram Spark is another option I used for one of my books but I found zero audience or success. I can't personally recommend the service.

2. Don't sweat the small stuff. It's easy to overthink every aspect of your book when you're in the thick of creating it but remember: *done is better than perfect*. Most people who are focused on perfection never finish their book. Stay focused on that first draft. It's a huge momentum boost when you complete it!

3. Don't be afraid to kill your darlings. If you aren't sure if something belongs in the book, it probably doesn't. Get a second opinion if you need to. You might be too close to the project to make a difficult decision. Again, it's a *"hell yes!"* or it's a *"no"*.

4. Hold yourself accountable. Set personal goals and deadlines. Map out your timeline because procrastination is your enemy. If you stop making progress it's easy to give up. That said, it's a marathon, not a sprint. You can easily burn out if you sprint to the finish line as I did for my September passive income challenge. Another tip is to announce that you are writing a book to friends, family, and on social media. This is a fantastic way to publicly hold yourself accountable!

5. Learn how to format the book and do it yourself. Trust me, this is a great skill to have if you intend to write more than one book. It'll save you time and money in the long-run to spend some time (and possibly money) teaching yourself how to format. If you are willing to spend, there are more expensive formatting options than Scrivener such as Atticus that are more user-friendly and offer unique formatting layouts.

6. Pay for an editor or editors. If you spend money on anything, spend it on editing! Be prepared to spend anywhere from $500 to several thousand. You may need a line editor to fix the bigger picture issue such as voice and style and a copy editor to find all grammar, punctuation, and spelling mistakes. Ideally you find someone that can do both!

7. It's okay to use AI for assistance. I didn't use Chat GPT for my book but there's no shame in doing so. AI can help you with your book description, keywords, editing, or even writing to help you push through moments of writer's block. Don't become overly reliant on it though, because people value books written by real people with a unique voice or point of view. Plus, you now have to disclose to Amazon if you used AI to write some or all of your book. I suspect that will hurt your visibility.

8. Spend as much time marketing the book as you can. Many first-time authors make the mistake of thinking the book is going to sell itself. It won't! That's why I'm putting preorders up two months before launch. I plan to spend the next 60 days promoting it and sharing all of those strategies in the next two chapters!

9. Don't write a book for the money. The reality is, you first book probably won't hit best-seller lists unless you have a large following or you're an total expert in book marketing. The reality is, you might break even, or worse, lose money. That's okay. Do it for the experience. Do it to find your voice. Do it to find your audience. Do it for the immense self-satisfaction. The money might come (I still earn money monthly from a book I wrote six years ago), but consider that a bonus!

10. If you're on the fence about writing a book, DO IT! Again, publishing a book is the most satisfying, gratifying, rewarding accomplishment. Seriously, the sense of accomplishment is priceless. 81% of people want to write a book at some point in their life. I'm guessing less than 0.1% actually do. *That could be you!* If nothing else, your book becomes the coolest business card. I often travel with a copy of my books in case I meet another author or even meet someone interesting next to me on the plane. Plus, it always comes up in job interviews!

SEPTEMBER RESULTS AND FINAL THOGUHTS

Obviously, I won't have sales to report for a few months when the book releases but my desired result was completed: I finished my book and it officially became available for preorder by the end of September. It releases on December 1st, 2023. It's out now if you're reading this!

I'm very proud of and excited about my new book "**Ready, Money Mindset, GO!**" It's teaches the reader how to develop a strong money mindset foundation so they can earn the financially free life they deserve. It's packed with critical lessons and tons of motivation and inspiration. At its core, it's really a book about how to discover more happiness in your everyday life, using money as a tool to get there. I think fans of my YouTube videos and books are going to love it and it will be tremendously helpful in anyone's financial journey. Truth be told, it's my favorite book of the four I've written so far. It contains my best content from a year and a half of deep research and consistent efforts. I succeeded in creating it because I stayed consistent and showed up daily. That's definitely a lesson in my money mindset book!

*Holding my 4 book babies! I love them all equally (*wink).*

Are you feeling fired up and think you can take on a similar 30-day book writing challenge? Lucky for you, there's actually a month annually when thousands of people attempt to do the same thing. It's called NaNoWriMo. That stands for National November Writing

Month. You can sign up and take on the 50,000 words in a month challenge at https://nanowrimo.org/. (I originally planned to take on my challenge in November to participate but I moved it up so I could spend October and November promoting it. Again, you'll learn all about product promotion next!)

Best of luck if you decide to write your own book. **Tell your story because someone out there needs to hear it!**

> *Questions for Reflection:* I'm going to put you on the spot and ask you, "What book is in your heart?" If you're unsure, think once again about a topic you know well enough to teach. Or, think about a story you've always wanted to share or an event you've always wanted to research or a historical figure you admire. Finally, reflect on what it would feel like to say you're a published author. What other types of passive income streams could your first book lead to? Hint: I wrote my book before I made YouTube content or wrote articles!

PART IV

Fourth Quarter

CHAPTER TEN
October: Organic Marketing

My mission to sell 1,000 copies of my book without spending money!

As any author knows (or learns the hard way), a book doesn't sell itself. With my book launch on the horizon—December 1st, 2023—I committed to a month of promoting my book so I can get it in the hands of as many people as possible on "pub day". You might be wondering, *"How is marketing a form of passive income?"* Based on my definition of passive income—earning a disproportionate amount of money for the time and effort put in—marketing, done right, has the ability to scale your orders and revenue well beyond the time and effort put in. If you can do it without spending a dollar, which was my 30-day challenge in October, that's even better!

It sounds obvious but nobody will buy your book or product or read your blog post, and so on if they don't know about it. You need marketing to get eyeballs, attention, and ultimately dollars. Fortunately, you don't have to spend money to sell your product or service. With the right strategies and a little creativity you can make your efforts go far, help your book rank at launch, and sell well over time.

This is my 4th book launch so I have a pretty good sense of what's possible and what's impossible. After some reflecting, I set three big goals for this book before I got started on outlining my organic marketing plan:

1. Build a book launch team of 50 members
2. Get 50 book reviews in the first 50 days after launch (preferably positive ones!)
3. Earn 500 book sales in the first 90 days

These goals are aggressive and would set personal records but, as you probably figured out by now, I like to set the bar high! I encourage you to set challenging yet feasible goals. Otherwise, it can be easy to give up when you fall behind. It's also a good strategy to establish baseline goals and reach goals. At a minimum, I wanted to earn 20 reviews in the first week after launch.

To get started, I first found all of my old marketing plans I documented in spreadsheets, Word docs, and a program called Trello. I wrote down all of my best past free marketing strategies and created a list of over 20 ideas for this book. From there, I ranked my ideas and started to tackle each of the top strategies one by one.

In the end, I was able to successfully implement 12 of my top 20 strategies. Here's a review of the 12 strategies I implemented throughout October, many of which you could leverage to sell any product you create! After, I'll share a list of 10 more free marketing ideas I'm hoping to tackle sometime before or shortly after launch.

TOP 12 ORGANIC MARKETING TACTICS

1. Create a book launch team

Building a team to support your book (or product) is incredibly valuable! It's the first strategy I'd recommend to anyone launching a book without a doubt. A launch team is a group of people that get a free advance review copy of your book in exchange for a review during launch week. I recommend you give this team around 30 days to read the book before the release.

Reviews are critical for a book's long-term success and a book launch team is one of the best sure ways to gain positive reviews at launch. With a goal of 50 reviews in 50 days, I need to know some or half of those will be nearly "guaranteed". I know from the past that about half of the people that sign-up to join a launch team typically fulfill their duties and leave a review. Therefore, if I hit my goal of a 50-member book launch team, that should turn into around 20-25 reviews.

How did I build my team? I asked! I posted on social media asking for help and these simple posts were effective. I asked people to email me or comment on the post and I ended up with close to 20 members from two simple posts on Facebook and Instagram.

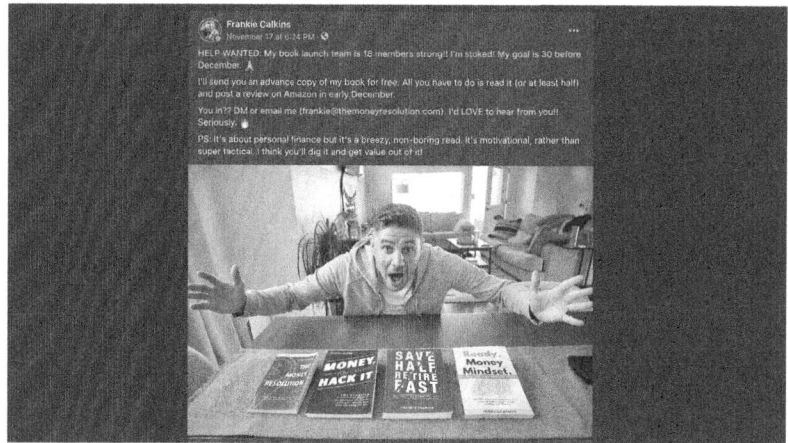

This Facebook post asking for help gained me 14 book launch team members!

I also emailed my list of 2,500 email subscribers. This led to 15 more people joining my launch team. If you have an email list, it is an incredibly valuable asset you should never hesitate to utilize, especially when you have a big new product or project to launch!

After people joined my team, I emailed them weekly with updates, the launch countdown, and gentle reminders them to read the book (or as much as they could) before my December 1st release. It's very important you stay in touch with your launch team weekly. Show them how much they mean to you. Make them feel part of a community and mission. Doing so also keeps the project and your big ask top of mind during their busy lives!

2. Post on social media & 3. Email your list

My book launch team strategy actually covered two strategies within it so I'll cover those both here together. You can and absolutely should use social media and your email list (if you have one) to grow your launch team, but you should definitely use social medial and email to promote your book as well!

I made several posts about my upcoming book on Instagram, Facebook, and X.com. I also sent two email blasts. One big tip for social media and email is to schedule your posts and sends! I plan to scheduled more posts and sends in November and during launch week. That way, I can focus on other strategies in the future.

If you don't have an email list, it's important to focus on building one with a lead magnet such as a giveaway or free "gated" content behind and email popup. People need a good incentive before they'll hand over information, especially if they know they are going to get more promotional email. As an idea, give away a chapter of your book in exchange for an email or offer book bonuses for signing up to be reminded about the launch.

4. Update your website or make one

If you don't have an author website, now is the time to make one! If you do have one, update it! I updated my site to include a popup you can't miss when you visit my site.

Popup on my site homepage: https://www.themoneyresolution.com/

I also added a link in the navigation on my site to my author bio on Amazon where my preorder was prominently featured. For my site, I use an all-in-one web platform called Kajabi. It allows me to create popups, send email blasts, host my courses, build easy landing pages, and more. It isn't cheap though. I pay north of $1,400 annually for my site, which includes all the aforementioned features. But there are cheap, or even free, options out there!

For my first author site I used Wix. I also considered Squarespace. These web platforms have a basic version you can use for free. If you want additional features such as a branded URL or shopping checkout you can expect to pay $25 or more a month. These web platforms have lots of easy to use templates and drag and drop features to keep things simple for those of us that don't know how to code. Other site building web platforms I recommend are Wordpress or Weebly, but there's a bit more of a learning curve with those options. Otherwise, there's always the option to pay someone else to build your site for you!

5. Write blog articles

Speaking of author sites, you can blog about your book on your site. Take people behind the scenes, talk about what the book means to you, or even offer small excerpts. Personally, I love writing on the site Medium. So, to promote my book, I wrote six blog articles in October which included mentions about my book throughout. One article was short and sweet, asking people to join my launch team. Another one was the script to my book trailer, which I'll explain next. Another article was the book Introduction, and so on.

6. Create a book launch trailer

A book trailer is a fun way to talk about your book in video form to get people excited about it. At a bare minimum, it should be a video of you talking directly to the camera for two to five minutes. I've made two book trailers in the past. I went ahead and made another one for this book in October. You can watch my book launch trailer on the YouTube channel "Passive Income Resolution". You can find my first two book trailer examples on my first YouTube channel "The Money Resolution".

You can make a book trailer with or without a YouTube channel. For example, you can film yourself and post it on TikTok or other social media sites. The bonus of creating a book trailer is that it helps you lock in on how to message the book as it forces you to think critically about who it's for and what readers will get out of it.

If you don't want to show yourself on camera, that's okay! I was very creative with my "Money, You Can Hack It" book trailer. I created images in Canva and used them to make a slideshow in iMovie that I narrated over, never showing my face. Honestly, it's my favorite trailer I've made to date (Note to self: Do that for *Passive Income Resolution*!)

7. Post in communities

If you do post your trailer on YouTube, don't overlook the Community feature. It can lead to great exposure. Since it's a relatively new feature, YouTube is showing these Community posts often. They look more like social media posts in users' feeds with text and images only. You can also create polls, quizzes, and more with the

Community feature. It's a great place to promote your book or product and ask for book launch team members. In strategy #12 I'll share three more online communities you should consider!

If you don't have a YouTube channel, think of other communities you are a part of where you could promote your book. That could be a work forum, sharing it with a sports team or club you participate in, a nursing home or pet shelter you volunteer at, your local library, your church, gym, and so on! There are more places and more communities around you than you realize! It's fun to think how to reach a large audience digitally but don't forget to think local. People love supporting people in their own *literal* community.

8. Update older content to promote your new book

As I've probably mentioned a dozen times, I've made hundreds of YouTube videos in the past so I went back into older video descriptions and added a link to my new book. Instead of spending hours adding it to hundreds of videos (many of which don't get views anymore), I added a link to my new book to the top 50 most-viewed videos in the last 90 days.

If you've posted other content online, go back to your previous work and add a mention with a link to your new book. If you have previous books, you should cross-promote by updating a page in those books to mention your new book!

9. Earn free PR

I always reach out to the local paper and local magazines to pitch my new book (by a local author!) to be included as a potential article or feature. This time was no different. As I mentioned with strategy #7, I also reached out to organizations I'm a part of. Lots of organizations are looking for content for their newsletters and are excited to share good work from their members with their community. With past launches, I was able to get articles written about my book in two different magazines via cold emails! For example, my first book was the topic in Teach for America's article "How to Climb to Zero (Net

Worth)".

As a bonus, request your book at your local library. This might not lead to a lot of sales but it's just flat-out cool. I'll never forget the first time I came across my book at my local library! I checked it out and gave it a 5-star review in the system of course!

Checking out my first book from the library in 2019 was a surreal moment!

10. Add a video to your book description page & update your Amazon Author Central

To add a video to your book detail page on Amazon, go to your book detail page, scroll down below book details, then click "upload a video". It's easy to miss but a great feature! I uploaded my book trailer. If you didn't make a trailer, you could film a quick video using your phone and quickly talk about the book or take people behind the scenes. Explain why you made the book, who it's dedicated to, who would likely enjoy it most, or anything else! Be sure to create your

Amazon Author Central account and fill out your bio, add a headshot, and poke around for other features that could be useful (they're always changing).

Finally, you can make your Amazon listing stand out even more by using the Amazon A+ content feature. I added a few striking images I made via Canva to my listing explaining special features of my book. To add these, navigate to the "Promote and Advertise" section within your book listing in your Kindle Direct Publishing account.

11. Leverage Good Reads

If you didn't know, Good Reads is social media for the biggest book lovers. Users take reviews and recommendations very seriously on Good Reads. Reviews are often more critical and honest so it's common for review scores to be lower than Amazon review scores. You can run ads on Good Reads if you have money to spend. But, at the very least, make sure you have an author profile so you can claim your book! From there, you can run a giveaway, blog, create an event for your book launch, and lead a Q&A group discussion about your book.

Similarly, I also applied to get my book verified on Medium. This is a new feature for authors. All it took was a simple form and now it's featured on my profile permanently. Plus, I have a verified author badge. It's an easy, free way to promote my book forever for people who visit my profile on Medium.

Frankie Calkins ✦

Home   Books   Lists   About

Featured Book   See all (2)

Ready, Money Mindset, GO!: How to Transform Your Money Mentality for Financial Freedom, Happiness, and a New Way to Live Wealthy

Learn how to develop a positive money mindset so you can succeed on your financial freedom journey and live a richer, as in happier, life.

2023 · Frankie Calkins   ↗

You can find this on my profile: www.medium.com/@fcalkins

12. Post on Reddit, Quora, and LinkedIn

There are dozens of online communities you can leverage to promote your book but my top recommendations are Reddit, Quora, and LinkedIn. These sites take some effort and you should avoid being overly promotional but, done right, they can be very valuable for exposure at no cost. Be sure to offer value with your posts and responses first. Prove you're an expert or entertain. Then, promote your product when and where it feels appropriate.

I posted in the Financial Independence Reddit page where they encourage shameless self-promotions. I also repurposed one of my Medium articles and posted it on LinkedIn as an article. You may not have known you can post articles on LinkedIn but you can and should!

10 ADDITIONAL FREE BOOK MARKETING STRATEGIES

Those are 12 strategies I've already checked off my list that I recommend. Here are 10 more quick, free ideas I'm hoping to take on in the next few weeks you should consider:

Run a book giveaway. I mentioned you can run a giveaway on Good Reads. You can also do this on your own! This can increase awareness, interest, and help you collect emails to build an email list.

Host a book launch party. I did this in person at a brewery for my first book and online during the pandemic for my second book. Both were a success. It's especially fun to do in person so you can sign physical book copies but a digital book launch party has the potential to reach more people.

Send a copy of your book to influencers. Emailing or sending a physical copy of your book is another great way to try to earn some free press. This could be YouTubers, podcasters, or "bookstagrammers" on Instagram for example. Before sending your book, try to contact them via email or social media. Make sure they know you'd like to send them a book with no strings attached. Don't expect the influencer to promote your product (they'll be turned off by this) but, if they love it and it fits with their audience, they might!

Gather editorial reviews. You can add editorial reviews in your Amazon Author Central account. Ideally you can gather short blurbs from small to medium sized influencers or well-respected people in your network. Know a fellow author? Swap blurbs with one another to use!

Cross-promote with other authors. Speaking of other authors, build a network of author friends and share each other's books with your networks. Authors love connecting with other authors for the community support, but also for the book promotion support!

Utilize Amazon Vine. This is an Amazon program that can help you earn more reviews. It sounds like a great resource to use for authors. Only the top reviewers are accepted into Amazon Vine so these reviews stand out in your review section with a badge next to the user name, giving it more authority.

Go on a podcast tour. Many podcasters are always looking for guests to bring on their show, especially people who are experts in their field. Writing a book makes you an expert in their eyes (especially for nonfiction). Try sending cold emails to go on shows that can help you reach your target market. I got on my favorite podcast "The Stacking Benjamin's Show" to promote my first book by attending a local meet up and giving a copy of my book to the host when he was in town.

Enroll in KDP Select. If your book is exclusive to Amazon, you get access to KDP Select promotions such as countdown deals and free promotions after your book has launched. Giving away your ebook for free for a limited time is a great way to help boost reviews in the first month after launch!

Run a Price Promotion

Start a Kindle Countdown Deal or a Free Book Promotion. **Note:** Only KDP Select books are eligible. Only one promotion can be used per enrollment period.

◉ Kindle Countdown Deals
◯ Free Book Promotion

[Create a Kindle Countdown Deal]

TikTok. Create a TikTok account and promote your book in short videos. Use the hashtag #Booktok in the description. It's an incredibly popular topic and a great way to promote your book! In fact, I'm dedicating my December challenge to TikTok so there's a lot more to come about this platform for passive income!

Record your audiobook. This isn't a direct marketing tactic but there are some people who will tell you they don't read books—they only listen to audiobooks. Now you can sell to that person who might normally ignore your listing. If you skipped Chapter 5, be sure to read it so you know all the ins and outs of creating a compelling audiobook for passive income!

OCTOBER RESULTS AND FINAL THOUGHTS

In the end, I was able to build a launch team of 41 members, very close to my goal of 50! I was thrilled with this and it doubled my previous best launch team. Twenty of those members came from social media, and most were friends and family. Ten of those joined by reaching out directly after reading one of my Medium articles. The rest came from my email blasts.

In terms of my book launch trailer, 300 people watched it on YouTube. My five articles on Medium gathered more than 2,600 views and a dozen comments from people telling me they preordered the book.

I won't know how much my other free strategies paid off until my book launches in a month but it was a very productive month of promotions and the positive momentum has me excited to take on paid marketing next month. But I won't stop there. Marketing shouldn't stop the day your book goes live. Continue to promote your book for at least 90 days after launch if you have the time and energy to do so. This will help your book gain traction and rank well over time for your top keywords and target audience. At a minimum, focus on gathering reviews. In the long-run, those are more valuable than income shortly after launch.

Again, new book is called *"Ready, Money Mindset, GO!"* It'll show you how to develop a positive money mindset so you can discover financial freedom, happiness, and a new way to live wealthy (that's essentially the subtitle I eventually landed on). It's the perfect book to read after this one! Plus, it includes lots of passive income tips to build on what you're learning here. You'll also learn how to uncover your purpose, buy back your time, and more. I'd be thrilled and grateful if you picked up a copy. (Obviously I had to end the chapter on free marketing by inserting some free marketing. Always be promoting...)

> ***Questions for Reflection:*** *What communities (online or in-person) are you a part of that could be great places to promote your book or product? What strategies could you leverage to build an email list or social media following? I covered lots of great organic marketing resources and ideas. Which of them caught your eye and why? Finally, how could you most effectively build a launch team of people excited to support you and your project?*

CHAPTER ELEVEN
November: Paid Marketing

I spent $1,200 to promote my new book.
Did it become a best seller?

The end was in sight. Two months remained in my quest to build 12 passive income streams in one year.

For November, I once again leaned into marketing for my 30-day challenge, but this time it focused on paid marketing. If you can spend $1 to make $2, that's passive income and you would continue to spend $1 to earn $2 as much as possible. The question is, could I do that? It's certainly not easy. If it were, everyone would have figured it out by now! Even big businesses struggle to find the most optimal paid strategies.

The following is a case study about my paid marketing efforts to help me sell as many copies as possible of my new book *"Ready, Money Mindset, GO!"* Throughout November, I paid over a thousand dollars to promote the book in four focused ways. I'll detail each of these four paid strategies from lowest spend to highest spend. In the end, I'll share initial sales for the book shortly after launch. *Finally*, I have some real sales data to reveal! I might also have exciting personal news to share after that...

PAID MARKETING TACTIC #1: BARGAIN BOOKSY

Bargain Booksy is a paid book marketing website and it's one of hundreds of sites you can pay to promote your book on. The reality is, the book promotion website world is pretty overwhelming. It was difficult to figure out which site would be best to promote my book on for my December 1st launch. I went digging through all the corners of the internet (okay, mostly Reddit) and I documented all the recommended sites. Eventually, I found a trend as one site stood out to me that seemed well-liked and (crucially) affordable: Bargain Booksy.

> BookBub if you can get in, ENT (same), Bargain Booksy and FreeBooksy, Fussy Librarian. BKnights is cheap and often gives decent results, though it can vary.
>
> Book Doggy, Book Basset, Digital Book Today, Bknights, Free Booksy, Booksends, BookAngel, Book Goodies, Best Book Monkey, LitNuts, Book Raid, Buck Books, justkindlebooks, Dangobooks, Book Cave, Books Butterfy, Bookzzlee, BookStage, Pixel Scroll, Bargain eBook Hunter, Fussy Librarian, Bargain Booksy, BookLemur, PlanetBooks, Book runes, Crave Books, Reader IQ, Bknightse, BookHounds, BookDealio, Bookbub, eReaderNews, Good Kindle Readse, BookSoda, eReaderGirl, ContentMo, Awesome Gang, LitRing, Robin reads, Many books, ExciteStream
>
> I would do BookBub if you can get them to take you, **BargainBooksy** (or FreeBooksy if you're doing KDP Select and are using up your free days on the promo), Fussy Librarian, and Robin Writes in that order. Add BookDoggy when BookBub rejects you.
>
> Fussy Librarian, Robin Writes, BKnights

Notes from my research you can steal! In retrospect, maybe I should have tried Fussy Librarian as well.

I spent $35 to promote my new book via Bargain Booksy on my December 1st pub day. The promotion included an email to their list and a feature on their website. Overall, it was a good experience. It was easy to set up and they executed the promotion exactly as they said they would. I have no complaints, especially because it was only $35.

If you only have $100 to spend on marketing, it's probably a good idea to spend it on the three top book promotion sites you choose after research! Let me say it again in case you are skimming: **do your own research**! See what sites show up over and over again and choose from there. Your genre and price point might influence your decision as well.

Ready, Money Mindset, GO!: How to Transform Your Money Mentality for Financial Freedom, Happiness, and a New Way to Live Wealthy ($3.99) by Frankie Calkins: Discover the path to financial freedom, happiness, and wealth through a transformation of your money mindset! Learn how to prioritize your financial well-being, buy back your time, discover your purpose, and explore the secrets of a positive mindset. You have the power to shape your success and enjoy the life you deserve – learn how to unlock it!

This deal is good on December 1, 2023

My book promotion listed on Bargain Booksy's website

I should also note that it can be extremely difficult to gauge the success of a promotion with any of these promotional sites—especially if you were trying a dozen or more strategies (free and paid) at the same time as I was.

In the past, I had a lot of success when I was running a free book promotion in combination with a handful of these sites. No, you don't earn money from free book sales but I had nearly 600 free book downloads during one promotional period.

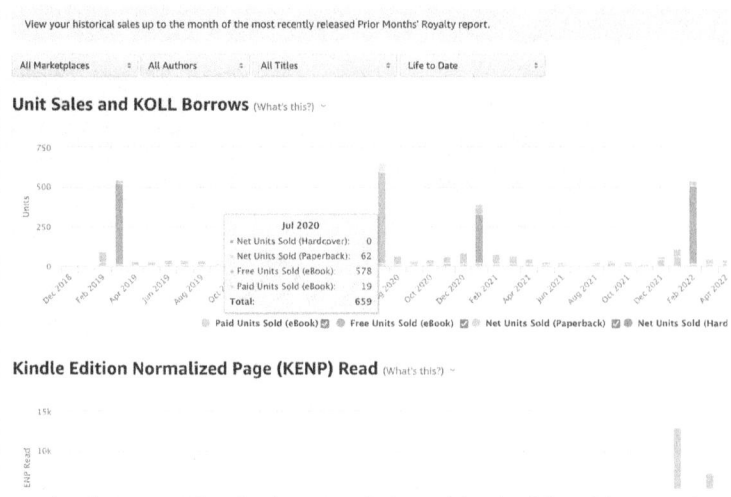

Example of one past free book promotion combined with paid promotion sites

How do I make money if I give away my book for free? Inside my books I promote my YouTube channels, finance courses, and other books throughout. Promotion sites combined with cross-referencing your upsells are a good way to get qualified readers exposed to your other work and offers.

PAID BOOK MARKETING TACTIC #2: AMAZON KDP ADS

This is a complicated subject to be sure but I'll do my best to simplify it. First, I watched dozens of YouTube videos and listened to a handful of podcast episodes to learn all about running Amazon ads for my book optimally. That might have been a mistake. It was information overload! Nobody seems to know exactly how to run successful paid ads but I will share the strategy I attempted and my top tips.

First, brainstorm and identify your optimal search keywords to target. There are free and paid tools out there to help you accomplish this. You might be wise to choose just a few keywords. Or you can select up to 50 or even 100. I recommend you start with around 10 and gradually reduce it to five or fewer based on your results. If you cast a wide net of 100 or more search terms to bid on, it will take a long time to gather enough quality data to learn from (or what data nerds like me commonly refer to as "statistical significance").

In the past, I ran ads for my previous three books so I spent an afternoon going through all the historical performance data by keyword and I found the top 100 keywords that were the most effective. (Due to a lack of education, I originally started with more than 750 words and phrases. **Don't** do this!)

Keyword	Column1	Match type	Suggested bid (lo)	Suggested bid (me)
fire movement		2 EXACT	$ 0.37	$ 0.41
retirement guide		2 EXACT	$ 0.39	$ 0.51
financial independence		2 EXACT	$ 1.63	$ 2.18
money guide		2 BROAD	$ 1.63	$ 2.18
millionaire mindset		2 EXACT	$ 1.73	$ 2.30
financial independence		1 BROAD	$ 1.65	$ 2.19
retire early		1 BROAD	$ 1.63	$ 2.18
financial independence retire early		1 PHRASE	$ 1.75	$ 2.34
money mindset		1 BROAD	$ 1.32	$ 1.76
retire early		1 EXACT	$ 1.56	$ 2.08
financial independence retire early		1 EXACT	$ 1.70	$ 2.28
retire early		1 PHRASE	$ 1.63	$ 2.18
save money		1 BROAD	$ 0.22	$ 0.35
save money		1 PHRASE	$ 0.22	$ 0.36
early retirement		1 PHRASE	$ 1.17	$ 1.55
early retirement		1 EXACT	$ 0.48	$ 0.64
financial independence		1 PHRASE	$ 1.65	$ 2.19
complete guide money		1 BROAD	$ 0.53	$ 0.70
complete guide money		1 PHRASE	$ 0.53	$ 0.70
retirement guide		1 PHRASE	$ 0.41	$ 0.54
millionaire mindset		1 PHRASE	$ 0.86	$ 1.66
save money		EXACT	$ 0.48	$ 0.63
money mindset		EXACT	$ 1.32	$ 1.76
retirement guide		BROAD	$ 1.63	$ 2.18
money mindset		PHRASE	$ 1.32	$ 1.76

Notes from my keyword research

Then I started a new "ad group" for all of my books, including my new book, using just these 100 or so winning keywords—which still might have been too many. For each keyword, you enter a bid amount from 10 cents to $3.00 or more. For the most part, I entered the lowest price in that range for each term, especially because I only earn $3 to $4 per book sale. For example, if I bid $2.00 per click and that earned me two clicks (that equals $4 spent), I'd have to convert one of those 2 clicks to break even. Most of my entered bids were from .25 cents to $1.50.

Then you set a daily budget. I set mine at $10 per book per day. You can also choose to pay more if you want your book to show up on the top of search results.

There's a lot more to it all but that's the gist. Here are screenshots of my results. Take a close look if you think you can make some sense of it.

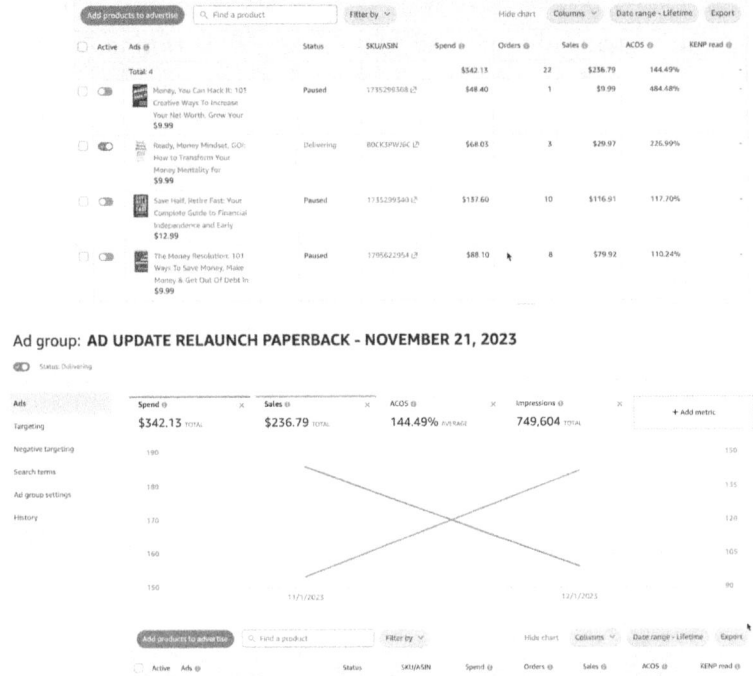

My Amazon KDP ads dashboards. Spoiler: I was losing money.

It certainly appears as though I'm operating at a loss—which means I'm losing money and that's bad. In research, multiple people pointed out that this ads dashboard actually *underreports* sales. If sources are correct, the picture might not be so bleak. For you, this uncertainty might keep you away from wanting to run ads in the first place! I wouldn't blame you if so.

Once again, it's hard to gauge if running ads was successful for me or not. When I compare actual sales from the Kindle Direct Publishing dashboards, I still suspect I'm losing money. On the other hand, there's something to be said about the exposure in general. You're only charged when people click on your sponsored advertisement. Sure, I paid hundreds for advertisements but hundreds of thousands of people were exposed to my book (in marketing terms, these are known as "impressions"). Perhaps, these impressions alone could lead to future buyers. It's hard to put a price tag on awareness! I mean that figuratively and literally...

Ultimately, I do recommend running ads for your book or product through Amazon for the first month at a minimum after your launch but DO YOUR RESEARCH. And only spend money you're willing to lose. If you're like me, it feels a lot like gambling even if you spend the time to learn. Monitor your advertisements closely and make adjustments as necessary. Some people swear by these ads. I can't do that but I am still very much ad-curious. That part is key. If ads don't sound interesting, you should probably stay clear of them. (*Paying someone else to run your ads is probably not going to be profitable either*)

Personally, I'm less concerned about making a profit because my book promotes all of my other products and services. I'm comfortable spending on marketing at a loss, especially for my learning and yours! Not to mention, it's an education book I'm passionate about so I'm thrilled by the idea of reaching and helping more people on my dime. It also helps that I work in marketing so I actually enjoy this stuff. #NerdAlert!

PAID BOOK MARKETING TACTIC #3: BOOKBUB

If you didn't know, BookBub is THE site all authors want to get their books promoted on. BookBub is where all the die-hard book lovers go to find hand-picked, highly recommended books on sale. BookBub's email list is reportedly above 20 million subscribers as of November, 2023.

In short, getting a BookBub deal feature is the closest thing to a "big break" for independent authors. Some authors sell thousands of copies of books during a deal period that costs a few hundred dollars. Talk about a good return on your investment! I've applied half a dozen times in the past to get a BookBub deal but I've been rejected every time within a day or two. Unfortunately, this time was no different.

However, this time around I also applied to be featured in the "New Release for Less" sub-section of the site. Ten days passed and I heard nothing. Then one night, I was relaxing on the couch with my wife when I got an amazing email from BookBub letting me know my book had been selected by the editors!

BookBub | *Partners*

Dear Frankie,

Congratulations! Our editors have selected your book Ready, Money Mindset, GO!: How to Transform Your Money Mentality for Financial Freedom, Happiness, and a New Way to Live Wealthy for a feature in BookBub's New Releases for Less email on 12/05/2023.

If you're interested in moving forward with this promotion, please click here to review and confirm the promotion details.

If you have any questions or concerns about the details of your campaign, please feel free to reach out to us and we'll be happy to help!

Best wishes,
BookBub Partners Team
https://insights.bookbub.com

Celebrations were in order! Or so I thought...

I was ecstatic! I accepted the deal immediately and paid the $300 fee with little to no thought. My book was releasing on December 1st and my deal would run on December 5th. This was perfect because that gave my book a few days to gather positive reviews so people would be convinced it was worth their money and time when they saw the promotion in their inbox.

Everything went to plan. I had a dozen 5-star reviews by the time BookBub emailed their list of readers interested in new "how to" and "self-help" books on December 5th.

I saw a spike in sales as you can see on this chart.

However, it wasn't as big of a spike as I was hoping for. This list was more specific and it was sent out to thousands of people, not 20 million. I probably sold around 30 copies of my book from the promotion. Since I make around $4 per book, that comes out to roughly $120 in income. I spent $300 for the feature. Therefore, I was once again operating at a loss.

I wasn't disappointed. In fact, I was super proud to finally be selected for a BookBub deal, even if it wasn't the coveted Featured Deal promotion. My book was featured on freaking BookBub and that had been a big goal of mine for years!

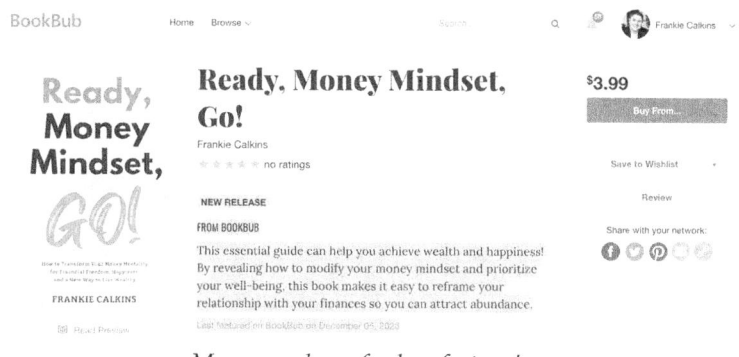

My new release for less feature!

From research, I knew to keep my expectations low about the "New Release for Less" feature because it wasn't going to their full list as a main featured deal. Plus, my book category isn't fantasy, sci-fi, or romance. Obviously I should write a steamy financial romance next where a couple joins finances and invests in sexy stocks in bed together...

Either way, I'm staying positive. You don't have a choice when you take on this many passive income challenges in a row. I'm thrilled that tens of thousands of people were exposed to my book and I hope this put me solidly on the BookBub radar. Perhaps it could improve my chances of landing a featured deal with the site in the future. The door feels cracked. I have more authority when I apply in the future because my book is listed on the site. I'm more determined than ever to break the Featured Deal door down!

PAID BOOK MARKETING TACTIC #4 NETGALLEY

In October an old boss saw some of my organic marketing promotions on social media and reached out to me. He was now working for a book publishing company and wanted to offer any advice he could lend to help me on my self-publishing quest. I took him up on his offer immediately. We chatted on Zoom for nearly an hour and he helped reinforce a lot of the organic strategies I was in the process of implementing. He also emphasized the importance of focusing on reviews over sales in the first 30 days after my book launches. Then, he shared a valuable resource I had never heard of to help me gain reviews: NetGalley.

According to their website, "NetGalley helps publishers and authors promote digital review copies to book advocates and industry professionals. Publishers make digital review copies and audiobooks available for the NetGalley community to discover, request, read, and review." In short, you can pay to list your upcoming or available book for book lovers to read for free in exchange for a quality review. My old boss said it's the resource they use for new books that they're publishing but also let me know it can be hit or miss, especially for my book genre.

It was simple to create my NetGalley account. From there I listed my book on the site. Getting it listed was a steep $600 price tag for a 6-month listing. After that, I hunted for ways to help my book listing stand out on the site and came across the promotion options. I went back and forth with the support team via email for a week before I finally landed on a promotion they were running 10 days before my book launch I could be included in it. I settled for the "Books Perfect for Gifting" category that was running the week of November 20th, 2024. Unfortunately, I missed out on the opportunity to run my promotion in my preferred weeks highlighting "Indie Reads" and "Practical Nonfiction".

This promotion ran me another $150, bringing my total NetGalley investment total to a whopping $750. It was a risk, but I didn't want to have any regrets looking back. Plus, I plan to write more books so it will be a valuable learning opportunity either way.

NOVEMBER RESULTS AND FINAL THOUGHTS

In the end, my book did earn the coveted #1 new release badge on Amazon which is always an exciting accomplishment and mini-goal! I can proudly say all 4 of my books have earned this badge of honor!

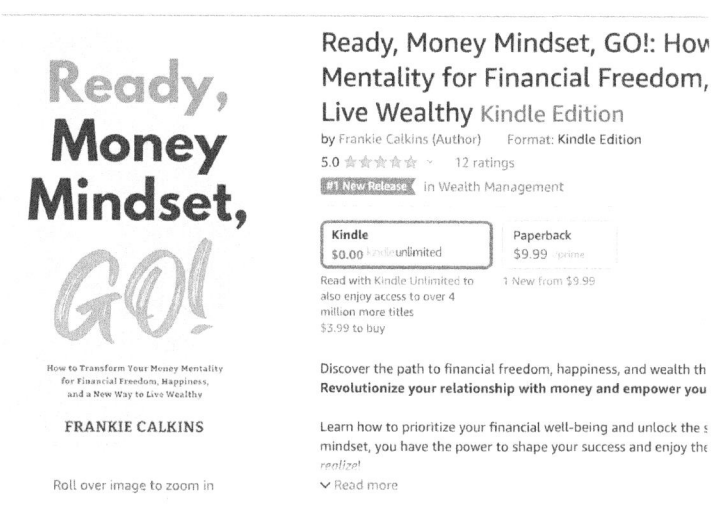

Nice to see you again old friend

It also nearly hit #1 in my category "wealth management". It peaked at #2 behind the book that inspired my book: "The Psychology of Money" by Morgan Housel (one of the most popular personal finance books). I'm perfectly happy with these results and minor victories.

My book hit #2 in my category on Amazon behind one of my favorite finance books of all time!

In total, I sold just under 100 copies of my new book in the first three weeks since pub day. That's not as many as I hoped for, but it's not a bad start and it's a little better than my previous two books. Plus, I didn't spend any money to create my book so these four marketing tactics were the only money I spent in total. Most of my books break even after a year and I understood the reality that the same might be true for this book, despite my big hopes and dreams.

As you can probably tell by now, it's extremely hard to make any real money as an independent, self-published author. There are a gazillion books making it near impossible to break through the noise. That's okay. Don't write a book hoping to sell a million copies. Write a book for personal satisfaction. Write a book because you have a story to tell or people to help. Write a book to find your voice, build your brand, and possibly sell other products and services you offer. Write the book that's in your soul because you know you have to.

As I said before, a book makes for the most memorable business card. It gives you authority. And again, it's incredibly satisfying. If you're like me, you might find it addictive as well. There's nothing like the build-up to pub day or reading the first reviews! Every time I look at my small stack of paper and ink on a shelf behind my office desk, I feel unbelievably proud of the stories I've shared and the lessons I've taught. It's the kind of pride a dad must feel when their kid aces a test or scores a goal in a sports game.

Speaking of, this feels like the right time to share I became a dad this month on November 1st! I'm especially proud of my latest book because it was dedicated to my new baby Wesley. I wrote it for him. I wrote it to inspire him in the future. If it happens to inspire somebody else, that's a bonus.

Dedication

For baby Calkins

Mind over all matters.
We can't wait to meet you!

If you take nothing else away from my three chapters about books and marketing remember this: **Write your book (or make your product) for the love of it. Do it for the right reasons. And never measure your success in dollars.**

Here are my results in dollars for the curious. I spent roughly $1,200 in total to market my book. I'll probably earn around $500 of that back in the first couple of months and over time I'll break even. I could even profit if I learn more about optimizing ads or land a BookBub Featured Deal. It won't be a huge money-maker but I love it and the early feedback was very positive. In fact, here's one review that's the perfect review in my eyes. It's exactly the message I was trying to deliver with my book:

>  Amazon Customer
> ☆☆☆☆☆ **Unlock Financial Freedom with Frankie's Wisdom**
> Reviewed in the United States on December 3, 2023
> In "Ready, Money Mindset, Go!," Frankie Calkins offers transformative insight into mastering your mindset to gain financial freedom. The book guides you on how to think about money, as opposed to how we've been conditioned, emphasizing the control we have over our success. From the profound impact of an abundance mindset to the revelation that taking back our time (our most valuable asset) is the true goal of mastering money, each takeaway is a stepping stone toward a new way of living wealthy. Frankie doesn't just provide financial advice; he crafts a guide that empowers, inspires, and leads to a mindset shift that can redefine your relationship with money. "Ready, Money Mindset, Go!" is a roadmap to financial happiness and freedom, allowing you to remember you're always in the driver's seat.
>
> One person found this helpful
>
> Helpful   Report

I also love this sentence another reviewer included as part of their review:

> *"I would be surprised if someone read this book and didn't walk away fired up to be their best (financial) self."*

I wanted to make a difference with this book. Mission accomplished. This book is currently my favorite book I've written. I know I've become a better writer and this book includes lessons that go well beyond personal finance. And who knows, maybe all my books so far are auditions for an agent and eventual book deal from a publisher. It's a dream of mine to reach a wide audience. (I often fantasize of seeing my book in an airport. I'd cry and melt into a puddle of gratitude if that ever happened!)

I know these results were more build up than pay off. I too wish the results were different. That all said, I genuinely hope you feel more encouraged than discouraged. Gradually, then suddenly you can succeed in this business. Your first and even second book might flop. But your 3rd or 10th or 20th might get shelf space next to mine in the airport.

Merrily we roll along to my FINAL 30-day passive income challenge: TikTok. After that, I'll provide a summary of all 12 challenges with full results one year after this year-long challenge concluded.

> ***Questions for Reflection:*** *How comfortable do you feel spending money to promote your book, product or services? How can you determine the right budget? How will you measure success for each of your marketing efforts? Do you think it's best to spend your marketing dollars before launch to build hype, at launch to gain early traction, or over time for sustained promotions?*

CHAPTER TWELVE
December: TikTok

I made 90 TikTok videos in 30 days to try to go viral

I did my best to stay away from TikTok over the years. I don't know what turned me off about it exactly. Perhaps because it seemed to target a teenage demographic—most people associate it with viral dance challenges videos after all. It also didn't seem good for our shrinking attention span. Plus, there has been talk about banning it in the US (if this is the future and it's banned, I assure you, something will take its place). And, of course, social media can be a time suck in general so I don't use a lot of it. In fact, I found a statistic that said the average TikTok user opens the app 20 times a day. As of December 2023, TikTok was the second most downloaded mobile app globally, trailing only Instagram. Maybe the reason I resisted it was because it was so damn popular!

On December 2nd, the day after celebrating my pub day, I grabbed my phone. I took a deep breath before opening the app store. I typed in "Tick Tock" like an uncool dad that embarrasses their kid all the time. I eventually found the app and installed it. The final challenge was on. But what the hell was I going to use it for? And what would I do about a username?!

WHY TIKTOK FOR PASSIVE INCOME?

Regardless of my reasons for avoiding it, I'll admit I've always been curious about TikTok. I've heard it's relatively easy to get a lot of views quickly. The marketer in me wondered if those easy-to-attract eyeballs could be used to help sell products. If nothing else, I could use a good laugh or two during the cold, wet, snowy month of December.

It also felt fitting to bookend my yearlong passive income project with short-form video projects. Back in January, my original passive income challenge was to monetize a YouTube channel by creating 4 YouTube Shorts a day. Short-form video wasn't a strength of mine going into the year but I wanted it to be a strength coming out of the year. I knew I could leverage my January experience, plus research, to give myself a shot at having one viral video. My strategy: create 3 TikTok videos a day for 30 days. Sure, I made 4 a day in January but that was on a platform I knew, without a baby to care for or the holidays to take my focus away.

After some quick research I decided getting monetized wasn't my goal. It sounded nearly impossible, especially in 30 days. The requirement for the partner program was 10,000 followers and 100,000 views in the last 30 days.

Instead, my focus became to start a new account and profile dedicated to promoting my 4 personal finance books—especially my September creation *"Ready, Money Mindset, GO!"* One viral video about the book or mentioning the book could help me sell dozens, perhaps hundreds of copies. One viral video became my goal for the month. Lots of authors appeared to be seeking out the same strategy. Here's how I set out to do it...

#BOOKTOK EXPLAINED

Lucky for me, there already was a massive corner of TikTok dedicated to books for book lovers. I always wanted to know where all the book lovers lived on the internet and I appeared to have hit the jackpot. Apparently, #BookTok is a big deal and influencers on TokTok have a massive effect on the book industry. The hashtag and trend of sharing favorite books by top creators is so popular that many bookstores and book sections in big box stores feature a stand of "as seen on #BookTok" books that have gone viral on the platform.

I did recognize one key problem for me: Those books all went viral because of BookTok readers who review and recommend books. It's users with huge followings that react to books, give audible or silent reviews, share their book haul, rank their favorite book of the month, share quotes, and more.

#BookTok videos on my TikTok feed

Immediately I wondered if anyone had ever mentioned any of my books. I quickly created my account @frankie_calkins_author (I saw other authors used this username format) so I could search my name and all of my books.

No results.

No surprise. I'm a nobody indie author. And by now I'm fully aware that personal finance isn't a sexy topic. It's not romance, mystery, or fantasy. *THOSE* are the categories that go ultra viral via

#BookTok.

MY SIMPLE IMPOSSIBLE PLAN

So, it was up to me. It was up to me as the author to make a new account and try to post compelling content about my book and book topic "money mindset". To get a boost in book sales, I felt confident that *one* viral post was my best path to success. All of my research from an author perspective backed up this idea. I knew from YouTube that consistency is key. I vowed to myself not to miss a day, even though I had no idea what to do on Day 1.

I got right to work. Per usual, it started with an idea session. I made a brainstorming list of all the video content I wanted to make. For the most part, they would be my version of popular posts I saw and other ideas from research. Perhaps I could ride trends within #BookTok and otherwise. Here's my initial brainstorm list I came up with after about 90 minutes of poking around the platform.

TIKTOK VIDEO BRAINSTORM
- How I published a #1 best selling book for $0 in 30 days (no AI)
- Ranking all 4 of my books…
- POV: When reviews for your new book reviews start to come in
- Would you read a book that ___
- Read parables from book
- My favorite chapter is my new book is…
- Silent book review of my 4 books
- POV: The moment you find your book is at the library
- POV: The moment your book hits #1 best seller
- Book #5: Topic Reveal
- Revealing my rejected book title ideas
- Library haul (including my book!)
- Today I googled myself and found something crazy!
- How to get your book in bookstores… (put it there, walk away)
- Best way to read my book: chapter a day for daily dose of inspo
- Why I cut 15 chapters from my book
- How I organized my nonfiction book chapters
- My favorite lessons from my new book
- My book is: The Psychology of Money + Happy Money
- My book bonuses: YouTube videos and 101 lessons in the back
- All the money books I own

HOOKS
- Use thumbnail words
- POV
- Would you read a book that…
- Best book about money (hide it)

OTHER IDEAS
- How I created a 45 member book launch team (clip from video?)
- My 12 passive income streams in 12 month challenge
- Best book about money is…
- How to create A+ content on Amazon page
- Why my goal is to retire early: you get 47% of your life to live

My original TikTok idea brainstorm in my master Google Sheet you can download for free: https://bit.ly/passiveincomesheet

Would this be another case of great planning, but bad execution? Here's how my videos and the month went week by week.

Passive Income Resolution

Week 1

First, I posted myself reacting to seeing my new book hit #1 best seller using trending music. Crickets. Then I went to my planning list and picked out the idea to rank all four of my books. Obviously, I chose my new book as #1. That earned over 500 views within an hour or two so that was encouraging. Next, I posted one of my most popular YouTube Shorts and it hit 800 views within an hour. Very encouraging! But it didn't mention any of my books—it was a story about learning a tough money lesson as a kid. It was a fun video I personally love, but a bit off-topic.

I knew I needed to post about my book so I took a minute from my book trailer and posted it and once again, I earned over 800 views.

My first 10 videos averaged 450 views!

A problem arose a few days in. My wife and I had planned to take a staycation at a nearby cabin with baby Wesley. We were going a little stir-crazy watching an infant and not leaving the house. I knew this would make it very difficult to make fresh content daily because my book ranking video took me a solid hour from start to finish to make. Plus, we had an infant to care for in a new place and the point of going was to find a little rest and relax (and maybe a few hours of uninterrupted sleep).

183

I came up with a plan. Before leaving, I found and organized all my best passive income YouTube Shorts from last January so I could post the best ones on TikTok. This would save me hours of time and effort during the staycation. Why reinvent the wheel when I simply didn't have the time? For the next few days, I re-posted YouTube Shorts and prioritized ones that mentioned my books. I sprinkled in a few new ones here and there.

Weeks 2-3

In week two I found myself posting one original a day and two YouTube Shorts. However, all this reposting of old content might have confused the algorithm. The content was unfocused. My videos were about many different personal finance topics and many videos were very different in tone and style.

I suspect this is the reason I hit the dreaded 250-view "jail" a few days into week two. I heard about this in my research. It's when most of your videos stop earning more than 250 views no matter what you do or try. Every video I posted for the next two weeks maxed out at around 300 views. It became pretty discouraging after nearly 40 videos with the same result. At a certain point, I stopped refreshing the app to see my metrics. I knew the answer.

From the middle of week 1 through week 2 I averaged 250 views.

By week three, I started posting about 70% "old" content, and only 30% new content. It became too frustrating to make new content, spend an hour on it, and still hit the same 250-view cap. More frustrating was that a few of my videos got flagged by TikTok. I wasn't sure why or even what that meant, but it seemed bad. I browsed the platform community guidelines. Perhaps my videos fell under the category of "unoriginal" and TikTok somehow knew these were YouTube Shorts reposted. Talking about money can also be tricky because TikTok prohibits spam and get-rich-quick schemes. Luckily, I was able to contest one successfully and that didn't happen again.

I made one key observation: my passive income content was driving more engagement, specifically likes. I went from 0-10 likes per video to 20–40 likes on most passive income videos. Therefore, I decided to move away from book content and money mindset videos. I decided to lean instead into passive income content exclusively for the rest of the month…

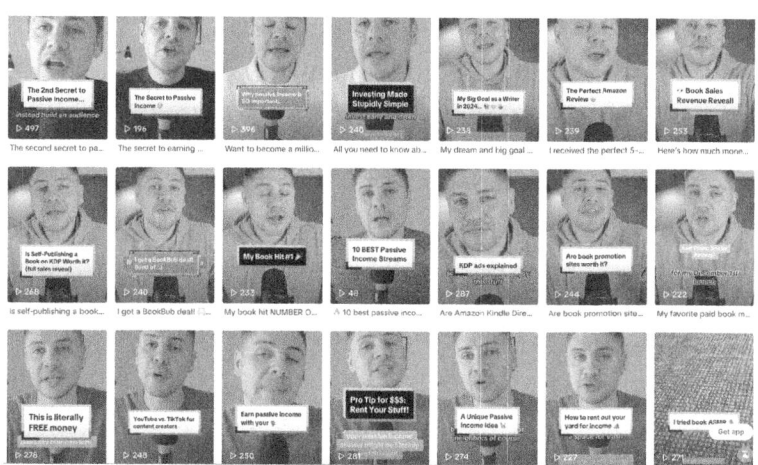

I leaned heavily into passive income videos and saw much better engagement

Week 4

At this point, I stopped making original content but I tried to give my old videos fresh edits like headlines and trending music. I also spent more time adding relevant passive income hashtags in the description (a variety of popular and less popular ones) and more time on the thumbnails and captions. I found posting in the evening was doing well so I posted more after 4 pm.

I continued to see improvement. In the final 10 days of December, I was consistently getting 20 or more likes per video, plus a couple of saves from people who liked it enough to stash it away (to re-watch on a rainy day I suppose). Plus, I started to get comments on videos. To be fair, half of them were crypto spammers, but that's better than no engagement...I think. I was also gaining around 3 followers with each new post, which was roughly 10 followers a day!

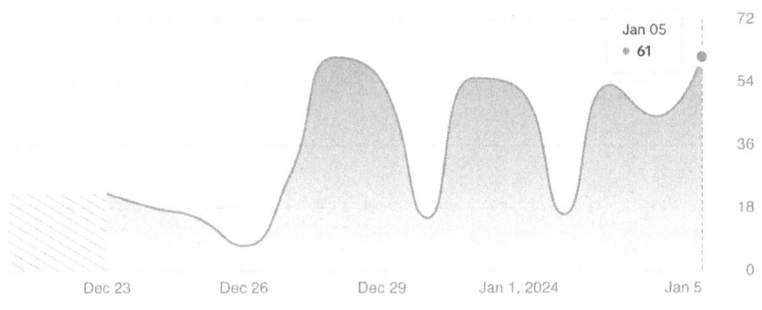

My daily boost in likes!

10 MISTAKES I MADE YOU SHOULD AVOID

Looking back at my original video brainstorm there were some great ideas in there. I failed to make two-thirds of my video ideas. I regret not staying focused on those. They were based on research the app and what was working after all! I didn't let the algorithm help me find the right audience. I got impatient with poor results in the middle of the month. Obviously, I have some regrets, which brings me to the 10 biggest lessons I learned. These are my best tips if you're getting started on TikTok or any short-form video platform as a content creator. (But also, consider that these are tips coming from someone that didn't succeed on the platform!)

1. Make fewer videos. Trying to make three videos a day made it very difficult to want to make original content. I knew I didn't have hours a day to commit to this project so I should have pivoted to two videos or even one high-quality video daily. You need to be honest with your time and use it wisely. I wasn't so I didn't.

2. Stay focused on your purpose for the platform. My original brainstorming list was very focused on what could work as an author. Instead, I started chasing results, leading me to change course. This defeated the whole purpose of trying to sell books by featuring them in most of my videos.

3. Niche down and stick with one topic. It's probably okay that I posted content from YouTube but I should have only posted videos about developing a strong money mindset, the topic of the book I was promoting. I should have provided samples of content from the book to help viewers learn in quick snippets, and intrigue them to want more.

4. If you have a product, try to find others to promote it. I could have offered free copies of my book to #BookTokers. I assumed most would charge a fee, but I didn't research this or try so I'll never know if that would have worked. Once again, I was limited on time so I chose a different strategy to create content rather than trying to create content rather than reach out to other content creators. It only takes a few minutes to copy and paste a short message on the platform!

5. Only use one to three hashtags per video. Only now after the month is over do I remember a tip I learned early in research to only use a few hashtags per video. I was loading my description with 8-10 hashtags on most posts. I should have stuck with the same few tags for every video for algorithm consistency.

6. Followed people in you target audience. I noticed following people did lead to a follow-back on many occasions. I didn't start following others until the middle of the month. Knowing this, I should have taken the time to follow people who seemed to like money mindset and book videos. If it's an author account, only follow people who post about books, your genre, your topic or are authors themselves.

7. Only view and like videos on TikTok related to your topic. I'll admit I often got distracted by the app. I'd open it to make a video and 30 minutes later I'd find myself in an infinite doom scroll loop wondering where the time went. TikTok was very good and identifying my interests (apparently sports, office and desk setups, unique finds on Amazon, comedy, travel recommendations, and dogs). Train your algorithm! If you want to use TikTok personally, create a separate account for that.

8. Focused on comments and user engagement. I know from YouTube that comments are extremely valuable and they are the best way to improve your standing with the algorithm. I assume the same is likely true with TikTok. TikTok's goal is to keep users on the app for as long as possible. If you video inspires someone to leave a comment, that takes more time to do so. It also indicates it's a video people are talking about, literally. A unique idea, a controversial statement, a unique statistic, or a ridiculous story are all ways to inspire more comments.

9. Think hard about your username. Change it if necessary. I'm not sure putting "author" in my username was the right move. Perhaps @frankie-money-mindset or something related to the topic of my book would have been more appealing to others. Unfortunately, you can only change your username every 30 days and I only had 30 days for my challenge so I was out of luck. A memorable username is probably more important than anything. When in doubt, try something punny!

10. Make your profile private to friends and family. This was an interesting tip I learned early on but once again ignored. I don't know if it would have helped but the idea is TikTok makes it very easy to discover your friends and family. As much as you love them, you might not want them to be a large part of your following in the beginning. You want followers in your target audience. If you do so, TikTok will start to understand what type of person will like your content and more of that kind of person will see your videos.

DECEMBER RESULTS AND FINAL THOUGHTS

TikTok was a learning process. I struggled to push through and complete my goal, especially when the results weren't there. That said —I did it! I made 90 videos in 30 days. Right now you're probably thinking I didn't reach my goal of having 1 viral video and selling a gazillion books. And if you think that…you'd be right. In fact, it's hard to determine if I saw an increase in book sales at all.

Beyond my viral video goal, I also set attainable goals to reach 100 followers and 1,000 likes by the end of the month. I'm happy to report, at the end of 30 days I ended up with 124 followers and 958 likes. That's pretty darn close. It's still a win in my book, and this is my book!

frankie.calkins.author
Frankie Calkins (Author)

☐ Edit profile

155 Following   **124** Followers   **958** Likes

Author of "Ready, Money Mindset, GO!" & more. See it happen, make it happen!

In the final chapter you'll see if I accomplished my big goal of creating twelve passive income streams in one year over twelve 30-day challenges. Regardless, by the end of December I accomplished the first big part of it. I gave myself the opportunity to succeed because I worked my tail off and actually completed the challenge! No matter what, I accomplished the *do the work* part of what I set out to accomplish. In the next chapter you'll see if I earned the financial outcome I was hoping for.

My motivation all along was to have a story to share with you—a story that would help others figure out what to do, or in some cases, what not to do. In that sense, mission accomplished. I'm incredibly proud of myself for following through on such a difficult resolution and goal for the year. I rediscovered how committed and persistent I can be—it was the only way I was going to complete my twelve passive income challenges.

Thank you for reading this far and following my journey. Thank you if you watched any of my videos, looked at or purchased any of my products, or left words of encouragement online. I felt like people were following along, even if it was just a handful of you in reality. Throughout it all, I was excited to know others would follow along after it was finished in the form of this book. That kept me extremely motivated to finish this book to share it with people like you. So, again, thank *you*.

I feel immense gratitude and personal satisfaction so this mission has already paid off in that sense. But alas, it's time to reveal if all of this hard work paid off in a literal sense…

> ***Questions for Reflection:*** *Which of these passive income opportunities from the book so far are you most excited to try for yourself? Why is that? What ideas have you already thought of? Don't forget to write them down! As a reminder, in the Appendix I included an exhaustive list of 101 passive income ideas that require little or no financial investment!*

PART V

Recap and Results

CHAPTER THIRTEEN
One Year Later

Month-by-month breakdown and full income results

I did it. I built twelve passive income stream in one year. It was my most difficult New Year's resolution yet. For half of the challenges, I tried to recreate my past successes but do it faster and better. For the other half, I took on brand new passive income stream opportunities that matched my skills with my interests.

Before we part, I want to share a recap of my projects, my process, and my final results including two bonus passive income streams that added thousands to my bottom line. Without further to do, here are the final results 1 year after I concluded my year of passive income.

JANUARY: A brand new YouTube channel "Passive Income Resolution"

The Goal: Get monetized and earn at least $1 by the end of the month.

Since I had monetized a channel before with "The Money Resolution" (which took me 2.5 years) I wanted to take a new, different approach. I set out to get monetized by hopping on the YouTube Shorts bandwagon. Since Shorts were relatively new, YouTube had been promoting Shorts aggressively. Competing with TikTok has clearly become a priority for YouTube in recent years. I decided to make 4 YouTube Shorts a day for the month of January, which I succeeded at. I made 125 Shorts videos by the end of the month.

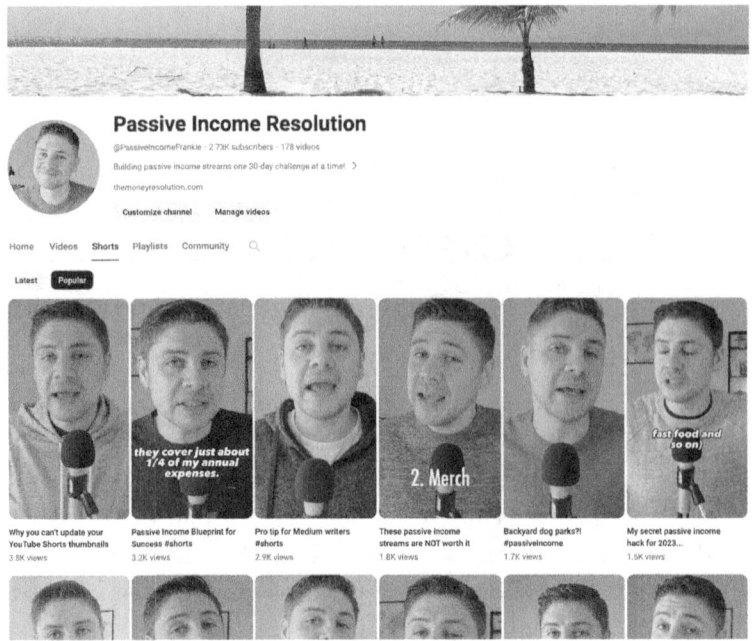

My new YouTube channel!

However, I made a big mistake. I failed to read the partner program requirements closely. To get monetized from YouTube Shorts alone you need 10 million Shorts views in the last 90 days. Looking at my data two weeks in (30,000 views), I knew this would be near impossible without a mega-viral video. I was forced to pivot and focus on long-form content. I tried to hack watch hours with two hour-long videos. I made weekly long-form updates. And I committed to documenting each challenge going forward.

At the end of the year, I did not get my new channel monetized. I easily achieved the subscriber requirement with over 2,700 (you only need 1,000). However, I only achieved 70% of the 4,000 watch-hour requirement.

Four of my 28 videos reached 1,000 views. My big win was one video that received over 20,000 views—my stock photography challenge video.

However, this story does have a positive ending. On July 28th, 2024 I became eligible for monetization, mostly thanks to my stock photography challenge video which crossed over 50,000 views by the end of 2024. I was officially monetized on August 4th, 2024 and I earned $180.88 by the end of that year, along with 4,089 subscribers.

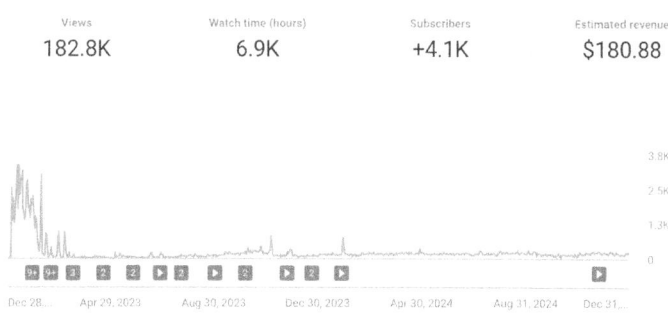

Final YouTube challenge results at the end of 2024

FEBRUARY: Alternative Investing

The Goal: Double my original investment of $500 within two years.

Alternative investments had always been interesting to me. I never committed because they seemed daunting to research and get started. Plus, I knew alts can be inherently more risky than traditional stock investing. I originally planned to invest $500 into one alt investment. However, during research, I got excited about a dozen opportunities I found across many different sectors and investment types. I pivoted and decided to invest $100 into five different alt investments. Here are the five alternative investments I chose:

- **Mainvest** allowed me to invest in a local business. I chose a new brewery restaurant north of Seattle.
- **Rally** allowed me to invest in collectibles. I loved navigating the app and looking at all the fun options, especially sports

memorabilia.
- **Vint** allowed me to invest in a wine collection. Vint is a competitor to Vinovest with a much lower minimum to get started.
- **Fundrise** allowed me to invest in real estate.
- **Prosper** allowed me to invest via peer-to-peer lending.

In late 2023 Mainvest shut down, which I assumed meant I lost out on my $100. Luckily, the restaurant I invested in sent me a check for $120, for a $20 profit. I sold my Rally investments for a $5 profit. Prosper, Vint, and Fundrise and still invested but the combined profits are around $21 so far. That means I've earned an estimated $46 in profit. The good news is I haven't lost any of my original $500! I also learned a lot and had fun doing so.

MARCH: Online Courses

The Goal: Update my first course, create a second course and earn $1,000 in passive income.

In 2020, I created my first online course Save Money Resolution, and decided to host it on my own website via Kajabi.

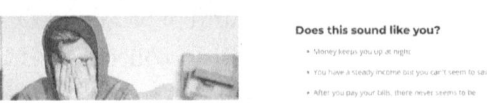

My course website

Since launch, I earned $451 in three years prior to this challenge. I rarely promoted it. I always had been happy with the course content but I wasn't nearly as confident on camera. So, I decided to refilm the entire 2.5-hour course for new and improved high-quality videos I would be proud of. I also wanted to see how my course would do on a site dedicated to online courses. After research, I decided to post my new and improved Save Money Resolution course on Udemy. Two weeks into March, both tasks were done.

In the final two weeks of March, I attempted to make a brand new mini-course. Choosing the topic was difficult. I remembered I had several videos about Medium that had a lot of views and interaction. A Medium mini-course became my answer.

Most people were interested in getting started and making money so I combined the two and called it Medium Income Quickstart Masterclass. It turned out to be roughly an hour in length over 5 modules. The course takes students from total Medium beginner to earning money in 30 days or less. It includes all my best tips, tricks, hacks, and resources. It's on my site and Udemy.

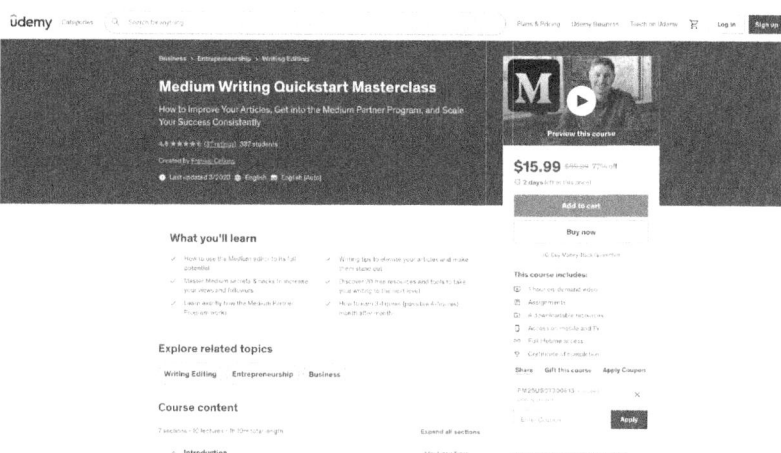

My Medium course on Udemy. Udemy wouldn't let me use the word "income" in my title.

So far I've earned $1,677 from my two courses across two sites. My

Medium course on Udemy has a 4.8 rating from 53 reviews and it earned a badge as the top reviewed course on the topic. I'm very happy with my courses, the feedback, and the income results so far!

My income dashboards via Udemy and Kajabi

APRIL: Stock Photography

The Goal: Make at least $1 from original stock photos online.

My revenue goal was not ambitious because I knew next to nothing about stock photography. I was simply looking forward to learning and improving my skills. I was most excited about this challenge and it turns out, others were too. My two stock photography video recaps were two of my most watched YouTube videos of the year.

Passive Income Resolution

Is Stock Photography Worth It? I Submitted 1,200 Photos to Find Out...
73K views • 1 year ago

I Tried to Sell Stock Photography as an Amateur...
3.3K views • 1 year ago

My stock photography results video was my best performing videos of the year by far!

I decided to take this challenge in April because we had a family vacation in Mexico planned. I loved the idea of documenting the trip with lots of high-quality photos and videos. Plus, I thought beautiful scenic shots of Mexico could be a hit online.

Each morning I got up before sunrise and walked about the community. I also took my camera with me everywhere we went as a group and made sure to take dozens of shots at every location. Back home, I went around my neighborhood and took another few hundred photos.

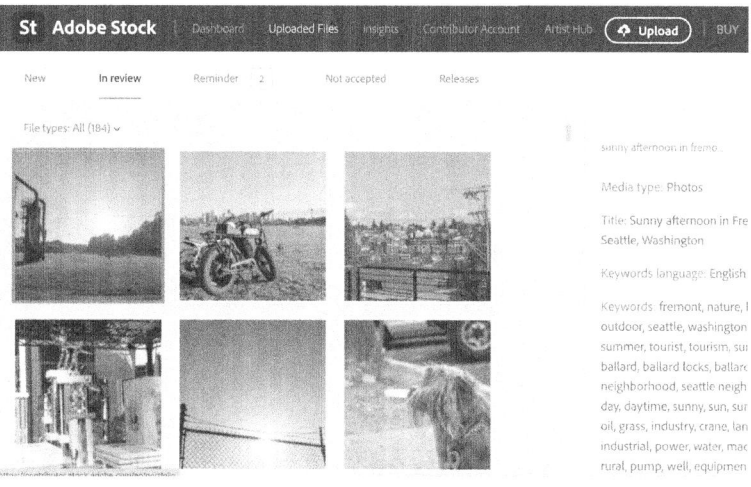

My portfolios on Adobe Stock and Shutterstock

All told I ended up with nearly 1,000 photos and videos. I decided to upload 600 of my best photos onto two different sites: Adobe and Shutterstock. In the end, I got 392 photos accepted and uploaded onto the sites. By December 2024, I had earned a combined $37.

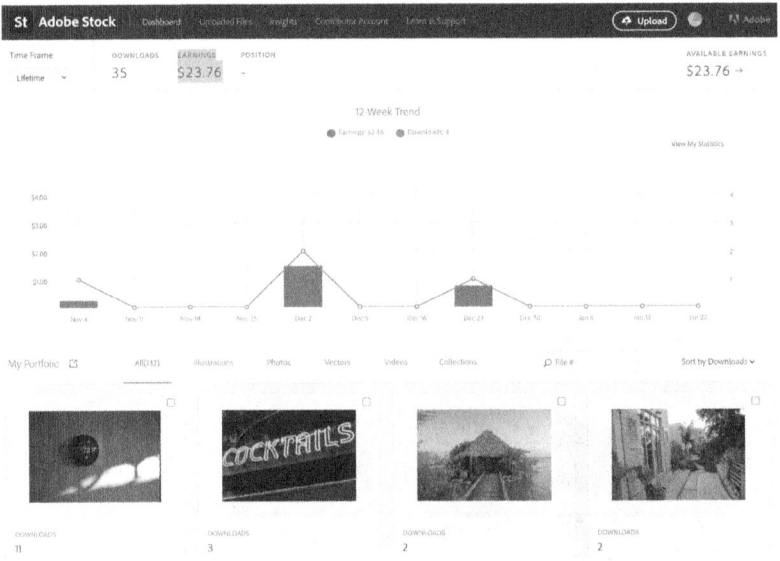

Monthly totals	4	$0.76	$0.10	-	-	$0.66	-
Date	Total downloads	Total earnings	Subscriptions	On demand	Enhanced	Single & other	Custom
12/02/2024	1	$0.10	-	-	-	$0.10	-
12/03/2024	1	$0.27	-	-	-	$0.27	-
12/04/2024	1	$0.10	$0.10	-	-	-	-
12/10/2024	1	$0.29	-	-	-	$0.29	-

My daily earnings reports from both stock photography sites.

It was a lot of work for that amount of earnings but I call it a win as a total beginner. I learned a lot about taking photos and editing photos. Plus, I got outside and got exercise so I had a blast. It's definitely a project I'll come back to in the future. I didn't end up uploading any videos so that would be next to learn about and focus on.

MAY: Voice (Audiobook)

The Goal: Produce the audiobook for my most recent book "Save Half, Retire Fast" and make a sale by the end of the month.

This challenge was all about tackling a tedious project I had been putting off for more than a year: finally recording my third audiobook. My two previous audiobooks taught me how difficult the process is, hence why I had been putting my third one off. More difficult this time around: my third book was close to 300 pages. My first book was 150 pages. My second book was 200 pages. So 290 was daunting. However, it was a great excuse to buy myself a new microphone as a business expense and off I went.

Instead of tackling the whole book in a one-weekend grind as I did before, I spread out the work. I put in one to two hours of work every few days. In the end, I regretted that decision because it felt like the project was always hanging over my head. Needless to say, I got the job done. My audiobook was uploaded by the end of the month and available on Audible roughly a week later. I earned $369.89 in passive income by the end of 2024 with little to no promotion.

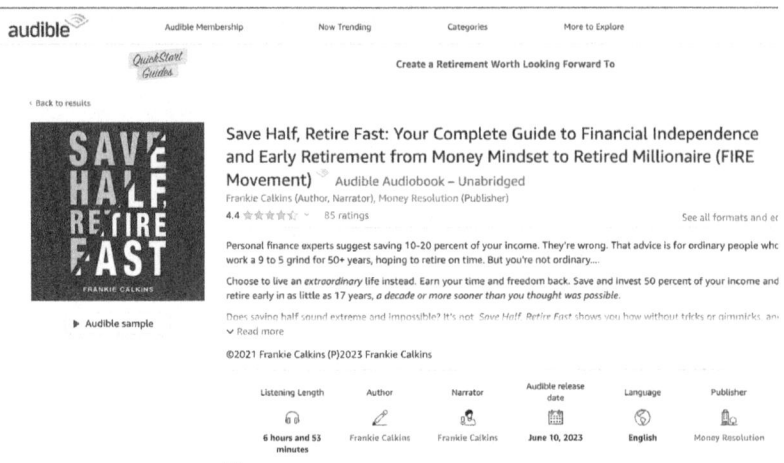

My audiobook product page on Audible

JUNE: Low-Content Books

The Goal: Produce 10 low-content books for sale on Amazon and sell at least 1 copy of each.

I thought about making no-content books such as blank journals or planners but I realized the genre was very saturated on Amazon. It would be nearly impossible to stand out from the crowd. I landed on low-content books instead because I wanted readers to learn something. I decided to post them under my name so they needed to be related to personal finance—the topic of my prior books.

I brainstormed a big list of ideas, ranked them, and got to work. Technically I outsourced some of the work using ChatGPT. Leveraging AI was a big reason I went the low-content book route. It was a good excuse to use ChatGPT for the first time and learning continued to keep my challenges fun for me.

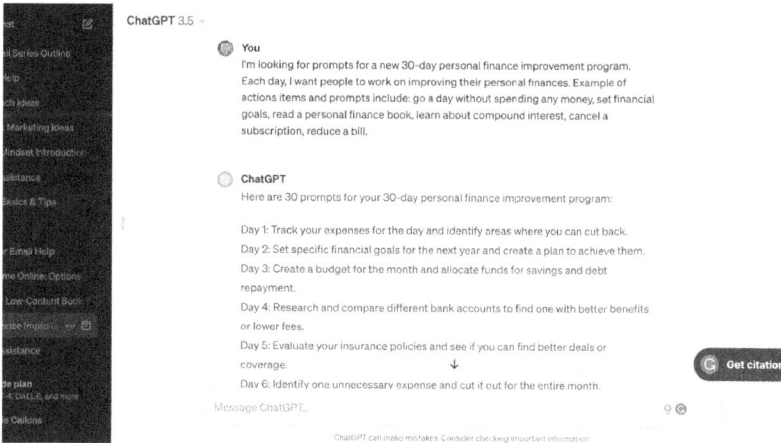

A prompt to help me organize a low-content book. I only wish there was a great free AI tool for making all the individual book covers!

In the end, I made a handful of guides for my courses and books, a list of things to do in early retirement, a budget planner, a 30-day money guide, and more. Sales-wise… they flopped. Again, I didn't promote these at all and the sales reflect that.

Book Title	eBook royalties	Print Royalties	KENP royalties	Total royalties	Total royalties USD
7 selected books	$0.00	$17.07	$0.00	$17.07	$17.07
101 Things to Do in Early Retirement: An Inspirational and Interactive Dream Life Activity Guide for the Financially Free (FIRE Movement)	$0.00	$13.32	$0.00	$13.32	$13.32
Master Your Money in 30 Days: A Comprehensive Financial Transformation Program for Smart Saving, Investing, and Debt	$0.00	$3.75	$0.00	$3.75	$3.75
101 Life-Changing Lessons About Money: An Inspirational Personal Finance Notebook for Doers, Dreamers, and Action-Takers	$0.00	$0.00	$0.00	$0.00	$0.00
Money, You Can Hack It Notebook: our companion guide to increase your net worth, grow your wealth, and have fun along the way	$0.00	$0.00	$0.00	$0.00	$0.00
Save Money Resolution Course Workbook: Your companion guide to saving your first (or next) $10,000 faster than you thought was possible	$0.00	$0.00	$0.00	$0.00	$0.00
The Money Resolution (Official Notebook): Your Companion Guide to Save Money, Make Money, and Get Out of Debt in 1 Year With 101 Money	$0.00	$0.00	$0.00	$0.00	$0.00
The Ultimate 3-Year Budget Planner and Tracker: Ignite Your Financial Growth and Transform Your Net Worth with Precise Income	$0.00	$0.00	$0.00	$0.00	$0.00

My KDP sales dashboard

I sold a total of 4 copies from 2 books and I earned $17.07. I also earned a 1-star review from one of those "book" sales. This was my first big fail of the year. A year later, I no longer recommend this passive income opportunity.

JULY: Affiliate marketing

The Goal: Get a channel sponsor and get approved as an affiliate partner with 10 brands.

This is a complex topic to cover quickly but here is the gist in five steps:

Step 1: I needed to get approved and accepted into as many affiliate programs as I could. I was accepted into Commission Junction, Awin, Impact, and Ascend. I was rejected by Share-a-Sale and FlexOffers.
Step 2: I created a list of roughly 100 dream partner brands—products I use and businesses I admire.
Step 3: I researched to figure out if these brands have an affiliate program and, if so, which affiliate platform they used.
Step 4: I applied to dozens of brands individually via these platforms.
Step 5: If accepted, I tried to figure out how to promote partner products and services to earn passive income.

In the end, I was accepted by 11 brands and I got two brands to formally sponsor a video in July (Vint and Unagi). I earned $1,338 in commissions in a 17 month period, plus a free electric scooter from Unagi to review and discuss on camera.

IMPACT		CJ		Share a sale - Declined		FlexOffers - applied to join! Denied	
Unagi - Impact	Accepted	Honey - CJ		Applied 7/20	Minted (20% commission, she	Haven Life	ht
Vint - Impact	Accepted	Ally - CJ		Applied 7/20	Warby Parker - Shareasale	https://www.s Alaska airlines	ht
Empower - Impact	Accepted	Discount Mags		Applied 7/20, ETSY		applied on 8/ Prosper - Flexoffers	ht
Puffy	Applied 7/19	Redbox		Deactivated account		MasterClass - Flexoffers	ht
Bulletproof	Applied 7/19	Fandango		Applied 7/20		Haven Life	Fl
Fanatics	Applied 7/19	Costco		Applied 7/20		Ben Bridge	ht
Yeti - Impact (applied)	Applied 7/13	Google domains		Applied 7/20			
Canva - Impact	Applications c	Brooks		Applied 7/20			
Minted		Dollar Shave Club		Applied 7/20			
		Herman Miller		Applied 7/20			
		Nike		Applied 7/20			
		Sonos		Applied 7/20			
AWIN		Rakuten		Has own / Other		Finish Research	
Dinnerly - Awin		https://www.a	Udemy - Rakuten	https://partner	Kajabi - has own	https://help.k Apple Podcasts	
Pawp - Awin		Nike		Rakuten	MoneyMade - used previously	Experian	ht
Fiverr - Awin (approved)					Grammarly - applied!	https://gramn Shopify	ht
					Dodo Fetch - Reach out, revoked, Ascend/P Spotify		ht
AvantLink					Lulu Lemon - Applied	https://shop.l: Brooks - Sovrn?	ht
Evo		AvantLink				Nike	ht
						Blue Nile	ht
						Puffy Mattress	ht
						Fandango	ht
							ht

My Google Sheet tracking all of the brands I applied to with outcomes

AUGUST: Cashback Credit Cards

The Goal: Open two or more new credit cards and start earning cashback.

The first seven months of very hard challenges were starting to take a toll on me. I sought out a simple challenge for August I could turn into an easy win. After all, August was my birthday month and I wanted to enjoy the sunshine in the Seattle area as much as possible before it gave way to our six months of doom and gloom. I landed on passive income from credit cards.

I have several travel credit cards but I didn't have any cashback credit cards. I reflected on my biggest spending categories and the stores I shop at the most. This led me to two cashback cards to apply for: Amazon Prime Visa and the Costco Anywhere Visa Card.

We spend a decent amount at Amazon and a good amount at Costco already. With a baby on the way, we knew spending at both of these stores would increase in the years to come. Both cards came with zero annual fee, a non-negotiable for me. With the Costco card I now earn 4% back on all Costco purchases (it's 2% for the card and 2% for being an Executive Member). With Prime Visa, I earn 5% back on Amazon purchases.

Don't overlook credit cards as an easy way to earn passive income with regular spending annually—as long as you are very responsible with them! In 16 months since applying for these cards I have earned $555 in cash. Admittedly, I typically spend the earnings at Amazon and Costco but a win is a win!

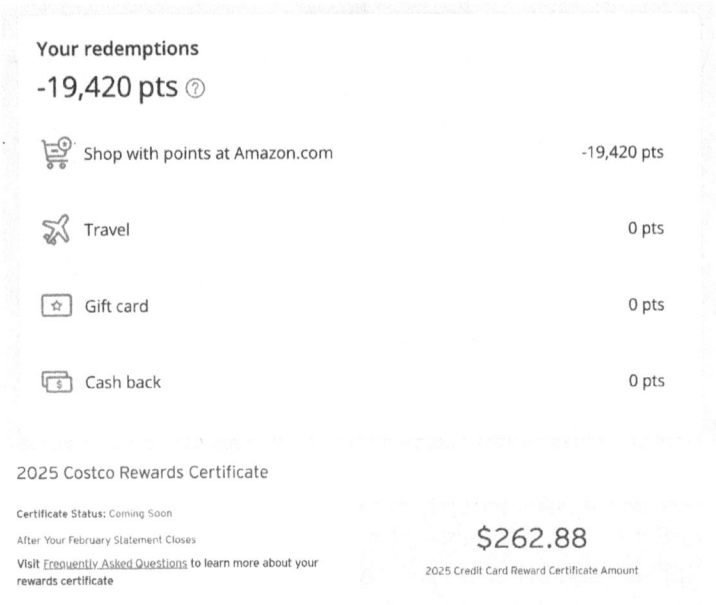

Our Amazon and Costco cash redemptions so far. We also earned $76 from Costco on our 2024 rewards certificate.

SEPTEMBER: Self-publishing via Amazon's Kindle Direct Publishing

The Goal: Write my 4th book in less than 30 days and make it available for preorder by the end of the month

By the end of 2022 I knew I wanted to write a money mindset focused book in 2023 so I made it a challenge. I wanted to take it on in November because that's NaNoWriMo month which stands for National Novel Writing Month. I pivoted to September to ensure I had more time to promote it while it was for sale as a preorder.

I had been sitting on a book outline for over a year. It wasn't a typical "how to money" book. It was a "how to think about money book". I spent most of 2022 making money mindset videos on YouTube so I had plenty of content already written. In fact, I turned dozens of those YouTube videos into articles on Medium so I had polished chapters ready to go!

I decided to create my book without help from others for the first time. I organized my chapter ideas, wrote my Introduction and Conclusion, and I spent two weeks editing. Editing is a grind so I pretty quickly regretted not hiring help! I eventually landed on the title *Ready, Money Mindset, GO!* I also took on the book cover design and here is how it turned out:

Proud book father!

I love this book! Even though I created it in less than 30 days, it was a year and a half of work in the making. It was a book that came from a place of passion. This book lays the foundation that inspires you to care about financial literacy, goals, financial freedom, and a continuously pursuing it. Of course, it's the perfect book to read after this one!

OCTOBER: Promote my new book without spending money

The Goal: Earn 25 book reviews in the first 90 days.

Throughout this book I've said that I wasn't as successful as I hoped to be because I didn't promote my work. I wasn't going to make that mistake again. I wanted to complete my book before October so I could spend two months promoting it until the release date: December 1st, 2023.

In October I took on organic, meaning free, marketing. (Yes, it might be questionable to call marketing passive income but it's my project so I make the rules!) To start October I made a list of 30 ideas for how to promote my book for free. From experience, I knew it was most important to focus on getting quality book reviews. This gives the book more legitimacy and helps boost overall book sales over time.

To earn reviews, I created a book launch team. This meant getting a group of people excited to read my book early and for free in exchange for a review the week of launch on Amazon. I set an ambitious goal to get 30 people to join. I ended up with 45! I found these book club members via friends and family on social media, my email list of 2,500 subscribers, and posting on Medium asking for help.

In the end, I earned 15 book reviews the week of launch and that grew to 22 with a 4.9 star rating by the end of 2024. That's the best rating of any of my books!

	A	B
1		
2		Book trailer. Made 2 versions for both channels. Promote video as an ad?
3		Street team / fan club - up to 18 members!
4		Write Medium articles
5		YouTube Videos / Community post
6		Add book to description to most popular video/articles
7		Email marketing blast
8		Post big announcement on social media
9		Send to Patreon subscribers
10		Contact local media: ST, TNT, Tacoma/Seattle weekly, Libraries, BECU
11		Request book at local libraries
12		Claim book on Good Reads
13		Get book verified on Medium
14		Post on Reddit
15		Add book to more categories - need to call (up to 10)
16		Update Amazon author central and add YouTube trailer to detail page
17		Add popup to site
18		Amazon super URL
19		Amazon Vine
20		Get on podcasts to discuss
21		Bonus landing page on site
22		Run a giveaway
23		Book launch party
24		

The the full list of organic marketing actions I took, plus some I didn't get to.

NOVEMBER: Promote my new book with a $1,000 marketing budget

The Goal: Sell 1,000 copies of my new book in the first 90 days.

Before I could get started promoting my book with paid strategies and a $1,000 budget, we welcomed our first son Wesley into the world in the afternoon of November 1st. I was elated, consumed by him, and losing sleep daily but it was easily the best day of the year (and my life). I worked on paid marketing when I could but I was obviously distracted for good reason!

In the end, I promoted my book via a promo site Bargain Booksy, via Amazon advertising, via NetGalley, and on BookBub. BookBub was a big break when it was selected by BookBub editors to be featured as a New Release for Less. BookBub is the top book site for book deals so that was a thrill! That said, it didn't pay off as much as I had hoped.

Was all this organic and paid marketing worth it? Was I

successful? Again, I got to 15 reviews much faster than usual. My book was featured on freaking BookBub! I did earn the coveted #1 New Release badge on Amazon. I peaked at #2 in my book's category behind *The Psychology of Money*, the book that partially inspired mine. And I love what I created. It's my favorite book to date.

How did it sell? Mixed results. Just over a year after release it has earned 183 sales equalling a total of $465 in revenue. Since I spent roughly $1,250 to promote it I'm in the red by $785. I'll likely break even in a year or so. Then, all sales will become profit. Eventually I'll create the audiobook that can also earn revenue as you learned about in Chapter 5.

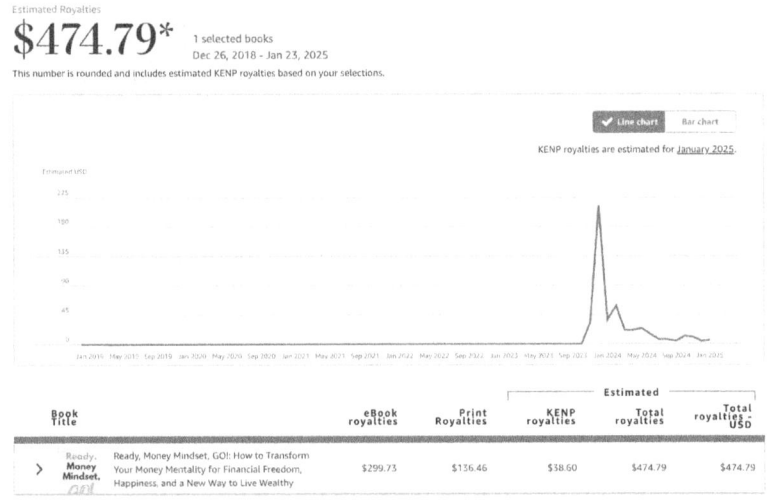

Royalties earned in the first year after the book released.

DECEMBER: TikTok

The Goal: Have one video go viral that mentions my book so I could sell 1,000 copies

TikTok had been on my radar for years so I finally gave it a go. I wanted to end the year with something fun. I didn't set my goal to get into the partner program because it sounded nearly impossible according to the terms. I was also exhausted and losing sleep due to baby Wesley!

Instead, I learned all about #BookTok and decided to leverage TikTok as another way to promote my new book for 30 more days. I created an author TikTok handle, committed to 3 videos a day, and got to work. Committing to three daily videos turned out to be biting off more than I could chew with a newborn. A week in, I started reposting old YouTube Shorts to get by. Before I knew it, my account became more about passive income via old Shorts from my January project than it was about my book and money mindset.

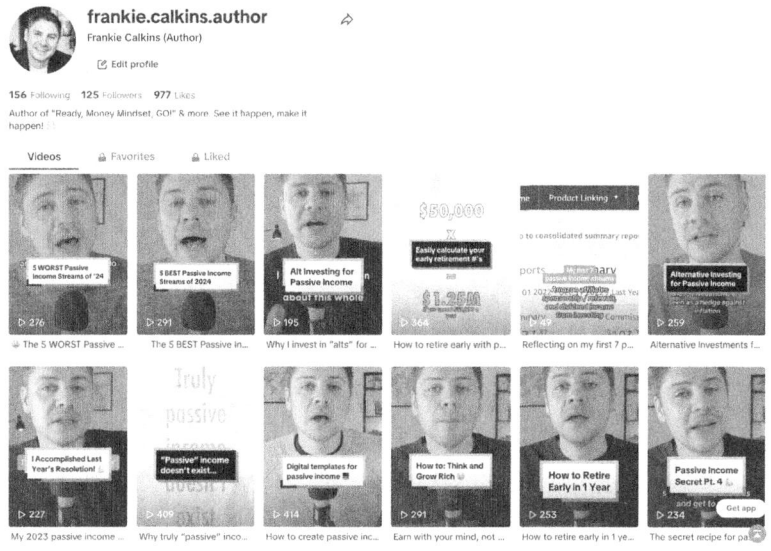

My TikTok page: https://www.tiktok.com/@frankie.calkins.author

In the end, I ended up with 125 followers and close to 1,000 likes on my videos. I learned the hard way TikTok is not a great way to promote your own book or product unless you have a lot of time and energy to commit to it. The real trick is to get your book or product in the hands of TikTok influencers who often go viral because word of mouth is powerful on the platform. If I had focused on that strategy, instead of making my own content, I would have been better off.

BONUS STREAM #1: Patreon

In the beginning of this chapter, I mentioned two bonus passive income streams I created. The first was a Patreon I started back in January. I peaked at 7 Patreon subscribers and earned $203 over a 12 month span. Eventually all subscribers cancelled after I stopped posting in early 2024.

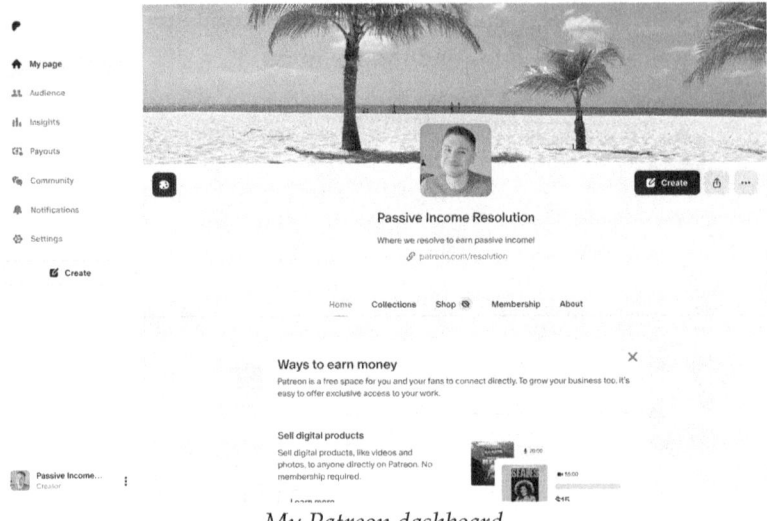

My Patreon dashboard

Patreon subscribers got access to my passive income Google Sheet I kept updated month by month, early access to video scripts and videos, and more! If you also want access to my document with all of my research notes, tips, thought processes, results, and more—you can get it for free at https://bit.ly/passiveincomesheet

Passive Income Resolution

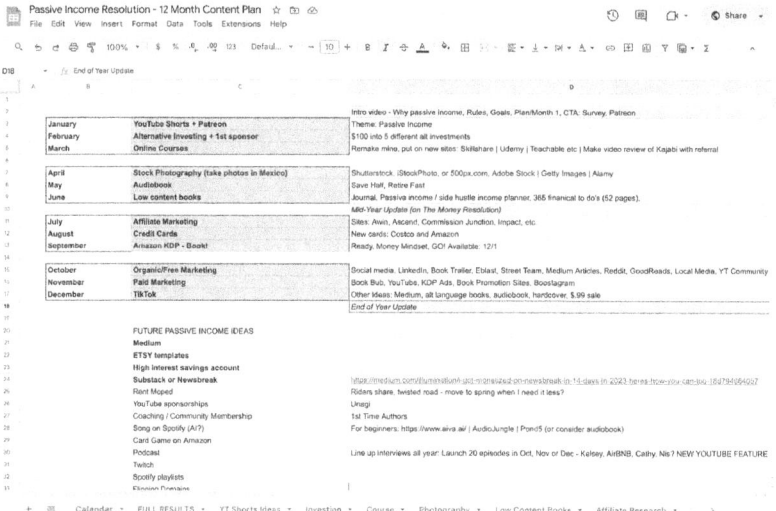

My planning document with all of my research and best ideas!

BONUS STREAM #2: Medium

I may have saved the best for last! My final passive income stream was Medium. For years I had been turning each of my YouTube videos into polished articles on Medium. 2023 was no exception. I posted 33 articles on Medium throughout 2023. Those specific articles earned $1,861 over a two year period. Two articles in particular earned $1,023 combined.

Is Stock Photography Worth It? I Submitted 1,200 Photos to Find Out!

· 9 min read · May 4, 2023

3.7K 58

Lifetime
May 4, 2023 – Today · Updated every 24 hours

$542.76	7.5K	4.5K	61%
Earnings	Views	Reads	Read ratio

Is YouTube Worth Starting? I Made 125 Videos in 30 Days to Find Out!

· 9 min read · Aug 31, 2023

1.8K 27

Lifetime
Feb 2, 2023 – Today · Updated every 24 hours

$479.82	8.4K	4.92K	59%
Earnings	Views	Reads	Read ratio

My top two articles from 2023 earned over $1,000. The 80/20 rule strikes again!

FINAL RESULTS

Passive Income Resolution

PASSIVE INCOME TRACKER 2023-2024

		Source 1	Source 2	Source 3	Source 4	Source 5	TOTAL
JAN	YouTube *(Partner Program)*	$181					$181
FEB	Alternative Investing *(Mainvest, Rally, Prosper, Vint, Fundrise)*	$20	$5	$8	$11	$2	$46
MAR	Online Courses *(Kajabi, Udemy)*	$273	$757		$631		$1,677
APR	Stock Photography *(Adobe, Shutterstock)*	$13	$24	$16			$37
MAY	Audiobook *(Audible)*	$370					$370
JUN	Low Content Books *(Created 8, only 2 earned sales)*	$17					$17
JUL	Affiliate Partners *(Awin, Ascend, CJ, Impact)*	$70	$60	$1,063	$145		$1,338
AUG	Cashback Credit Cards *(Amazon, Costco)*	$216	$339				$555
SEP	KDP Self-published Book *(paperback, ebook, Kindle unlimited)*	$475					$475
OCT	Organic Marketing *(trailer, fan club, articles, social, email, etc.)*	22 reviews, 4.9 stars					-
NOV	Paid Marketing *(Bookbub, BargainBooksy, Net Galley, ads)*	BookBub feature					-
DEC	TikTok *(book sales / partner program)*	158 followers					$0
	Bonus 1: Patreon	$203					$203
	Bonus 2: Medium	**$1,861**					**$1,861**
						TOTAL:	**$6,760**

Expenses: $1,200 paid marketing, $300 microphone
Plus, free product, referral income

215

Hint: Turn your device or book sideways.

By December 31st, 2024 I earned $6,760 from my passive income streams built exclusively throughout 2023. I set out to build 12 passive income streams that could earn monthly with little to no future effort for years to come. In the end, I actually earned passive income from 22 individual sources! Of course, I also spent around $1,500 on marketing and a new microphone. **That means my overal profits were $5,260.**

Does that equal financial freedom? On the surface, no. However, this project wasn't solely about the earnings in the first year or two. Most months I built an ongoing passive income stream that will continue to earn income for years to come. The YouTube channel, alternative investments, book, articles, stock photos, credit cards, courses, audiobook, partnerships, and more will continue to generate income. I did the work once, now I'll continue to earn money with little to no effort going forward.

Most importantly, I set a big, time-bound goal and I achieved it. Very few people actually follow through with their New Year's resolution. I did, and then some! How did I do it? I thought through a challenge I was excited about, I broke it down month by month, I stayed organized, I documented my progress, I showed up daily, and I never gave up. I failed some months and succeeded in others but I am proud of the effort. A year later, I'm especially proud that I created this book to help you on your journey so you know what mistakes to avoid and what successes you can replicate! I hope you already feel motivated to build a passive income stream or streams. That, ultimately, was a driving motivation.

Do you need 12 streams of income? Probably not. In fact, I don't recommend taking the approach I took. Start with one passive income project and work hard on it for at least 90 days. Then re-evaluate, plan, research, and execute always keeping in mind your interests and your skills. Keep what works and ditch what doesn't. Follow your skills and interests. Set big goals and give yourself a set amount of time. I was in a hurry. You don't need to be!

Before I share my top learnings from the year and say farewell, I want to let you in on a little secret: Earning passive income can become addictive. Why? Because it can literally change your life. Done right, building passive income streams can absolutely lead to financial freedom and even early retirement. It's more possible than ever so I leave you with these final questions to consider...

> ***Questions for Reflection:*** *What could you do in a year if you focused on it and committed? How much passive income could you earn? What would you learn and create or make to help others that would make YOU proud? Is the future or right now the best time to commit to taking action? I think you know the answer to that!*

Conclusion
Learn to Earn

It wasn't all pretty but I scrapped and clawed and accomplished my second official "money resolution". It was an exhausting year. I had big wins, made a ton of mistakes, and learned a lot. There were many highs and several lows. It would be a massive understatement to say it was a year I'll never forget.

Here are the top 12 critical lessons I learned. I strongly believe these lessons are more important and valuable to you than my summarized research, step-by-step walkthroughs, or final results. This is the advice I'd give my closest friends and family about seeking passive income streams.

To discover passive income success, it's important to match your skills with your interests.

This is the #1 lesson I hope you take away from this book. To create a successful, long-term passive income stream or streams, you need to think critically about your skills and your interests. If you can find a project that marries those two together, that's your sweet spot. *That's where you'll find your big opportunity.*

Make a list of your skills and interests. Then research passive-income streams that merge the two. When an interesting one comes up, you might have that light bulb ah-hah *ringtones* moment—that's a reference to the Introduction if you're confused! You might uncover your unfair advantage. Use this "skills + interest" brainstorm exercise to help guide you to your next passive income idea. It also works in reverse: Give yourself this gut-check test when you find yourself excited about an opportunity. Ask yourself, *"Does it match my skills and interests?"* If you aren't sure, the answer is probably no.

Measure twice, cut once.

Brainstorm and research. Then research and brainstorm some more. *THEN* plan and execute. Yes, you can and will continue to learn as you go but that initial brainstorming, research, and learning is critical. If you plan to build your passive income stream over several months or a year, you may want to research for a full month before taking action and rushing into something in the wrong direction.

For most of my 30-day challenges, I focused solely on learning for the first full week. I was a sponge. I obsessed over articles, podcasts, YouTube videos, and books. Luckily, if your skills and interests align, you won't find it hard to want to research and continue learning.

I brainstormed what I knew. I took notes while I was learning. And I updated my brainstorm to rank my best ideas throughout. But I was never really done. When I hit a wall or a critical challenge I couldn't solve, I researched some more. This is why I created my YouTube channel in month one. If nothing else, I felt compelled to document every month on YouTube to help others with *their* research.

Don't fall victim to shiny object syndrome.

Here today, gone tomorrow. Tech changes. Algorithms change. Peoples' interests change. Pick something thoughtfully and carefully (as I just discussed), then give it a real go.

I set a ridiculously hard challenge to build streams in 30 days or less but I don't recommend doing it the way I did it. It's hard to find real success in just 30 days. You need to stick with something and see it through. There's always going to be a new, latest, best, lucrative passive income idea or opportunity but don't be in a hurry. Wait three months, six months or a year to jump on a new idea or concept. If you still want to pursue it, do so with focus.

Plenty of opportunities interested me over the years: Dogecoin, NFTs, flipping houses, and the app Clubhouse. All of those would have been a waste of time and probably money. Make your plan, and stick to it!

There are no shortcuts. You have to do the work.

There's nothing "passive" about passive income until you create the thing, find your audience, and build your systems to continue to support or promote it. I put in a TON of hard work every single month. Producing my audiobook was a 40-hour project. Meticulously editing 600 photos and adding 50 tags to each photo on two sites was even harder than learning to take great photos. Writing a book could take you years! If you're new to passive income, please understand it's not a shortcut to becoming wealthy. You have to match skills and interests, you have to learn, you have to focus, and you have to put in the time and effort.

While there are no shortcuts, there are helpful resources out there. In fact, I have one for you that I've mentioned several times… You can get my full research and planning sheet that walks you through my learnings and thought process for every project and study what I did. Get a look behind the scenes and snag this freebie that also includes my full month-by-month results! You can grab it at https://www.themoneyresolution.com/PIRbook

There's no such thing as luck.

"Luck is what happens when preparation meets opportunity." -Seneca

I truly believe this to be true when it comes to passive income. Even if you come across an overnight passive income success story, know that "overnight" almost certainly means months or years of matching skills + interests + seeking knowledge + learning from failures + taking many "shots on goal".

Even when I had a lucky moment or two on my passive income resolution journey (for example, my BookBub deal) I created that luck. I applied to BookBub six times before they said yes. I wrote a book in a month but only because I had written three before. Plus, I spent a year and a half creating content on the book topic on my first YouTube channel. When you're prepared from years of experience and armed with a great idea and strategy, you can get lucky. But that's not luck. That's preparation + opportunity.

It's not enough to build a product or service—you have to promote it!

By now you understand the importance of this because I spent two chapters dedicated to marketing and promotions. You must have a plan to spread the word and attract your audience. You can do this in a variety of ways. I spent a month trying to promote my book for free and another full month experimenting with paid marketing to promote it. I tried to build buzz about it before it even existed and had a full marketing plan before it was complete.

I'm a marketer by day so this part came naturally for me. But I have to emphasize the importance of marketing once again because I'd hate for you to do everything right but fall at the finish line because you didn't think about how to promote your product or service. Speaking of promoting…

Track your efforts.

What doesn't get measured gets missed, especially when it comes to marketing. For me, it was very difficult to say which of my book marketing efforts actually led to sales because I didn't track them. I regret not creating specific tracking links for each strategy and staying extremely organized. Instead, I tried a million things and hoped for the best (another strategy I don't recommend).

Pick three or four of your best promotion ideas and go all-in on them but track what works. Run A/B tests. Trial and error is okay. Then cut out losing strategies and lean into winning strategies. Trust me, not everything works. The 80/20 rule applies here: 20% of your efforts likely lead to 80% of your marketing success. For example, my big win was creating a 45-member book launch team that led to 15 5-star reviews shortly after my book launch date.

If it's not working, move on.

Don't be afraid to kill your darlings. At a certain point, it's okay to call it quits if something isn't working out and move on. If you gave something your all and the results aren't there (and no improvement is in sight), don't go down with the sinking ship. If it doesn't align with your skills or interests, abandon ship. Grab a life vest and get off the boat. Refocus. Readjust. Reflect on your skills and passions once more and find something new that you're excited about.

I did this more than once on my 12-month journey. One month I planned to start a Medium account from scratch focused on a totally new topic for me. I chose parenting because I was going to be a dad. I wrote an article and brainstormed several others. After a week of trying to start several more articles, I realized my passion for writing about the topic wasn't there. I pivoted. It was a week-long setback but at least it wasn't a wasted month or more.

Take days off to reset and find balance.

This is your reminder in case you haven't heard it in a while: You need balance in life or you can and will eventually burn out. Don't become obsessed. I always give myself Saturdays off from all work. I highly recommend the "one day off no matter what" approach. I started doing this back when I was a high school teacher.

Take a break when you hit a wall. You'll come back to the challenge or problem refreshed and more likely to think of a creative way to break through. Here's another reminder you might need to hear: Take a vacation if you haven't in a while. They are rejuvenating to the soul!

Document your journey.

This comes back to helping you track what's working and what's not but it's also about forcing you to stop and reflect. Plus, documenting your journey publicly is a good way to hold yourself accountable. Knowing I was going to share every project in a YouTube video was enough for me to push when I wanted to give up or was having a tough week.

I never closed my Google sheet that had my plan, all my learnings, and my notes about my wins and misses. I checked in with it at least every other day for a year and it was usually the first thing I saw when I opened my computer in the morning (don't worry, I minimized the window if it was Saturday!).

As a bonus, you might be able to turn documenting your journey into a new source of income. I documented my 2018 new year's money resolution and eventually turned it into my first book. This book is also the product of documenting my year-long passive income journey. Having it all documented made it impossible for me to *not* write this book!

Don't be afraid to ask for help.

I was, many times. I was stubborn about it. I didn't pay for help once. I didn't even pay for editors or a book cover designer for my new book for the first time. I thought I could do it all. That alone might be why it didn't sell as many copies of my book as I had hoped.

I did leverage ChatGPT for one project, but a robot does not replace human efforts intended to reach other humans. Use resources but leverage people as well. Sometimes it takes money to make money and that goes for paying for help. Work smarter, not harder.

On that note, don't hesitate to ask me a question. Email frankie@themoneyresolution.com if you'd like to get in touch!

You can learn a lot from 30-day challenges.

I recognize this contradicts myself a little but somebody might want to hear this: If you're at the beginning of your passive income journey, you may not know your skills or you need to develop them. You may not know your interest or which of your current interests is something you won't eventually tire of. You are the perfect candidate to experiment. Try something. Then try something else. Don't focus on results in 30 days. Focus on how you're feeling. *Does it feel like work or are you excited to work on it?*

Focus on learning and developing skills. Think about the long-term idea of working on this same product or service or house flip for years and years. *Can you envision it or not?* Your gut is more powerful for clarity than you realize but only if you jump into the fray and try.

Further, you have to make decisions very quickly when you only have 30 days. This can be a good thing to help you avoid analysis paralysis. Plus, deadlines inspire action. Imagine what you could learn and possibly earn if you committed for 30 days. The results might surprise you. They certainly surprised me time and time again in 2023!

Best of luck on your passive income journey. I hope you feel inspired to set your money resolution, whatever that means and looks like to you. You can change a lot in a year, including your financial life. But it doesn't have to be January 1st to set a one year goal!

As always, you can email frankie@themoneyresolution.com with any feedback or just to say hello. I also appreciate any feedback on Amazon in the form of an honest review if you're willing. Reviews go a long way in helping others discover this book.

Stay inspired. Take consistent action. Don't give up. One day, pay it forward. Then one day, enjoy yourself and relax. Frankie says. Just do it! (*If you know you know*).

Thank you. Good luck. And thank you again. I write my books and make my videos as if I'm talking directly to one person. I'm grateful that person was you.

> PS: As a self-published author, it can be difficult to reach more readers. If you got value from this book, an honest review on Amazon is the best way you can help me share value with others. Then browse my list of passive income ideas in the Appendix, watch some YouTube videos, and get to work! You got this!

Resources
YouTube Companion Videos

As mentioned in the Introduction, every chapter has at least one corresponding YouTube video I've created. Watching these will help reinforce the core concepts, provide visuals, and add to everything you've learned. Below are the playlists names with videos by chapter for your viewing pleasure. You will find these playlists at this URL: https://www.youtube.com/@PassiveIncomeFrankie/playlists. You can also find all of the videos in one place via the "Passive Income Resolution" playlist on the Passive Income Resolution channel.

Chapter 1 | Month 1: YouTube Shorts
Chapter 2 | Month 2: Alternative Investing
Chapter 3 | Month 3: Online Course Creation
Chapter 4 | Month 4: Stock Photography
Chapter 5 | Month 5: Audiobooks
Chapter 6 | Month 6: Low-Content Books via KDP
Chapter 7 | Month 7: Affiliate Partnerships
Chapter 8 | Month 8: Credit Cards
Chapters 9-11 | Month 9-11: Amazon KDP Self-Publishing & Book Marketing
Chapter 12 | Month 12: TikTok

Appendix
101 Passive Income Ideas

1. Start a blog on a personal website and sell ad space
2. Sell digital products on ETSY
3. AI pet portraits (example - https://www.pawtrait.art/)
4. Write Medium articles - see Chapter 13
5. Start a Substack newsletter
6. High interest savings account
7. Rent out your vehicles (Turo)
8. Invest in individual stocks
9. Invest in dividend stocks
10. Invest in mutual funds or ETFs
11. Invest your HSA funds
12. Alternative investing - see Chapter 2
13. Online coaching
14. Community membership
15. Make songs and put them on Spotify
16. Create a card game to sell on Amazon
17. Start a podcast
18. Twitch streaming
19. Create popular Spotify playlists that artists will pay to be featured on
20. Website domain flipping
21. Sell merchandise on sites on Teespring.com
22. Create and sell Canva templates
23. Gumroad templates or products
24. Payhip
25. Buy Me a Coffee
26. Start an OnlyFans
27. Become known enough to be listed on Cameo
28. Affiliate Marketing - see Chapter 7
29. Buy a sticker machine and sell stickers through Redbubble
30. Vending machine
31. Invent an app that makes money (example: sell phone background images)
32. Sell your app once it's making money
33. Create an affiliate based review website on a specific niche
34. Nebula
35. Rent out storage space (neighbor.com)
36. Create and sell ringtones - see Introduction of this book for more!
37. Credit card rewards and cash back - see Chapter 8

38. YouTube super chats, super thanks, and channel memberships
39. Instagram sponsored posts
40. Teachers Pay Teachers
41. Patreon - see Chapter 13
42. Sell a recipe book or workout guide - can be digital
43. Dropshipping Shopify store
44. A digital product Shopify store
45. Sell a product or service online
46. Online courses - see Chapter 3
47. Become an expert at paid marketing - see Chapter 11
48. Royalty exchange
49. Flippa
50. Create and sell a font
51. Create and sell image filters for Photoshop
52. Retail arbitrage on Amazon
53. Join Nielson and earn from watching TV
54. Airbnb property
55. TikTok - see Chapter 12, although I didn't succeed!
56. Merch by Amazon
57. Kindle Scribe templates
58. Farmland investing
59. Peer to peer lending - see Chapter 2
60. YouTube ads - see Chapter 1
61. Self-published ebook - see Chapter 9
62. Self-published paperback
63. Self-published hardcover
64. Self-published audiobook - see Chapter 5
65. Stock photography - see Chapter 4
66. Low-content books - see Chapter 6
67. Rental property
68. Buy and sell a business for a bigger profit
69. Advertise on your car via Wrapify.com
70. Rent out a spare room
71. Rent out your tools, snowboard, golf clubs, bike and more
72. Collect memorabilia via garage sales and sell them
73. Start a Certificate of Deposit (CD) savings account
74. Sell website templates
75. Sell stuff around the house!
76. Sell digital posters
77. Create a curated subscription box service
78. Bargain shop, then re-sell vintage clothes
79. If you're an artist, seek out commissioned pieces (increase your rates!)
80. License music, jingles, or sound effects

81. Pay someone on Fiverr to cold call your list
82. Make instructional videos
83. Cryptocurrency… if you have the stomach for it!
84. Pay someone to translate your self-published book into another language
85. Ask for a discount when you order just about anything!
86. Rent out parking space
87. Pet sit in your home
88. House sit for someone else. Work on passive income streams while doing so!
89. Purchase a billboard
90. Invest in royalties
91. Create greeting cards
92. Create a print-on-demand store
93. Rent out space via Peerspace
94. Help businesses bring in clients, earn commission
95. Use passive income apps such as InboxDollars and Dosh
96. Create a job board, charge for promoted listings and ads
97. Participate in a sleep study (or any study)
98. Create and sell 3D designs
99. If you're a student, sell your notes via sites such as Stevia and StudySoup
100. Start a gym empire
101. License your code if you're a software developer

ANOTHER SPECIAL GIFT FOR YOU

Medium Income Quickstart Masterclass
A Course for Writers Seeking Passive Income

Medium is my favorite writing platform and my mini-course (from Chapter 3) delivers all the tips and tools you need to scale your following and earn passive income!

You get 1.2 hours of video lessons, a PDF of all 97 tips, 20 free writing resources & tools, and lifetime access.

Get it 75% (!) off with code PIRBOOK
as a thank you for your purchase and support!

Automatically claim your offer at:
bit.ly/StartMedium

Made in United States
Orlando, FL
21 April 2025